GW00535824

WOOD YOU BELIEVE

VOLUME THREE

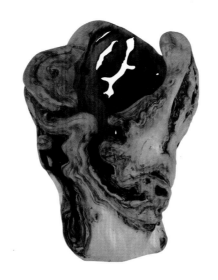

THE ANCESTRAL SELF

Blessings
Jim C.

Wood You Believe – The Ancestral Self.

Published by:
Jim Cogley
Bethel, Kilmore Quay, County Wexford
Ireland
www.woodubelieve.org

Copyright © 2007 by Jim Cogley.
Photogaphs © Fr. Jim Cogley
First Published 2007

All rights reserved. No part of this publication may be reproduced, stored in a retrieval system, or transmitted in any form or by any means, electronic, mechanical, photocopying or otherwise, without the prior permission of the copyright owner.

Design & typesetting by Maciek Zygadlo
pinguin@jamjar.com.pl
www.jamjar.com.pl

Printed in Poland

ISBN 978-0-9557110-0-8

Dare to climb out of your Family Tree!

This book is part of a trilogy with:

WOOD YOU BELIEVE

VOLUME ONE

THE UNFOLDING SELF

A JOURNEY OF SELF-DISCOVERY & HEALING
EXPLORING SPIRITUALITY AND PSYCHOLOGY
THROUGH HANDCRAFTED WOOD SYMBOLS

And with:

WOOD YOU BELIEVE

VOLUME TWO

THE EMERGING SELF

A JOURNEY OF SELF-DISCOVERY & HEALING
EXPLORING SPIRITUALITY AND PSYCHOLOGY
THROUGH HANDCRAFTED WOOD SYMBOLS

FOREWORD

$\mathcal{B}$ooks have a mysterious life of their own. A book that is just right for where we are at on our life journey has the capacity to bring light and new awareness and often seems to find us more than we find it. Even as the author, I feel that this book just found me and came through me rather than from me. It seemed to just want to be written. With the minimum of effort, in the middle of a busy schedule, and with amazing synchronicity it came together in just three months. The right stories, the right encounters and the right information all started coming the day I started writing. My vision for a book of healing, written from the Irish perspective, on this important subject has been more than met with divine provision.

This is a, 'How to' book interlaced with theory and stories. It is all about healing and is designed for the many who are attempting to understand who they are in relation to their past, especially their family history.

The Ancestral Self was written, not after an exhaustive study of all the available literature on the area of Family Tree Healing and other related topics, but rather from the experience of being drawn to work in this area for the past twenty-five years. It forms the second part of the much read *Wood You Believe* Series. Volume 1 was entitled *The Unfolding Self* and Vol 2 was *The Emerging Self.* In all two volumes symbols of wood are the medium that connects the human and the spiritual dimension, hence the title *Wood You Believe.* In 1998 following a brief appearance on the R.T.E. programme *'Would You Believe'* on the subject of *'Family Tree Healing'*, I was surprised by the large numbers of requests received from all over Ireland for more information on the subject. At the time my limited response was to prepare a brief information pack, which was forwarded to those who enquired.

Because it was impossible to accommodate all the requests to conduct family tree services in different parts of the country it became necessary to have a gathering once every month where people who were interested could travel, share their story, explore the subject at a deeper level, and the evening would then conclude with the celebration of the Eucharist. Since that time the first Friday of the month has been the regular date for such gatherings. Every month new people arrive while those who have been there previously are able to witness to the miracle of transformation that they have witnessed in their families resulting from family tree healing. As this work has progressed, experience has deepened and new insights have come my way.

Seeing the weight of intolerable burdens being lifted from so many has left me utterly convinced of the validity of this work. Results speak for themselves. It is also my reason for encouraging others to, where necessary, extend their horizons, learn about, be aware and if possible take part in this very effective area of the healing ministry. This book is an attempt to commit to paper much of my current understanding of the subject and hopefully in some way it will serve to meet the ever-increasing demand for more teaching on this fascinating area.

One section in particular that I deem to be of extreme importance and where I continue to witness many remarkable healings is that of Sibling Bondage. There is a current shortage of literature on the subject that reflects a serious lack of understanding of these issues of loss that affect so many. Hopefully what is written here will enable many more therapists and those burdened in this way to have eyes to see what may be at the root of problems and how these issues can be dealt with, particularly by cutting the ties that bind.

My intention is to present a clear and reasoned approach to an area of healing which is so often shrouded in mystery, distorted by religiosity, and occasionally viewed with suspicion because of inadequate understanding. Many of the questions, which have been raised over and over, will hopefully be addressed. As it is an area of ministry that is still very much in its infancy, any comments, stories or insights received from readers will be greatly appreciated and used to progress this work. To all who have contributed their story or allowed their story to be told I offer my sincere thanks. Ultimately it is only testimonies and stories such as these that give credence to this work and I am grateful for their enthusiasm and support.

Wood You Believe Volume Three

The Ancestral Self

Table of Contents

Part 2
Hauntings & Happenings   69

Part 3
Politics & Religion   91

Part 4
The Ties That Bind   111

Part 5
Prayers & Rituals For Healing   137

Acknowledgements

Almost all the pieces illustrated in this book represent my own work done over a three-year period. While many of the concepts are original, there are several that I have drawn from the work of other turners. These designs have been taken, and usually adapted, from a wide variety of sources such as books, exhibitions, and especially the magazine *Woodturning*. While I am deeply indebted to so many for their originality, it is impossible to always give credit where credit is due. I unreservedly apologize for any of these inadvertent omissions regarding either text or design, and would welcome these being brought to my notice.

The stories included are genuine and have arisen out of clinical and pastoral practice. In most cases names have been changed and details re-arranged but in a manner that preserves their essential truth. For literary purposes they have also been shortened considerably and a story that may have taken months to unfold is now condensed into a short paragraph.

I am deeply grateful to all who have helped in preparing the material for this publication, especially my editor, Áine O'Ceallaigh. Their advice and support has been invaluable.

The cover piece of Volume Three entitled *The Ancestral Self* is a nature design. It is made from olive wood and comes from Vilnius in Lithuania. In its contortions and distortions it reflects the troubled history of its country. It also reflects the wholeness that is the goal of Family Tree Ministry where fragmentation has given way to integration. For this prized and valuable gift I am indebted to Donal Wills now living in Barbados.

For the piece entitled *Ingrained Trauma* I am grateful to Stephen Whelan. This masterful work of art represents his first incursion into the rewarding field of working with bog oak.

Photo of Pax Sinnott taken from 'Wexford in the Rare Oul Times'.

To Joyce Rupp I am indebted for some of the material found in the section *Prayers and Rituals*.

To those who submitted their stories or allowed their stories to be written, my sincere thanks; your contribution and courage will make it possible for so many others to tell their story.

To the magazine *Irelands Eye* and in particular to its contributor J.J. Tohill I am grateful for the use of material contained in his article entitled *Holocaust to Vengeance*.

To David Furlong author of *Healing Your Family Patterns* I am indebted for the concept of the piece entitled *Ancestral Inheritance*.

Thanks to Simon & Schuster UK Ltd. for the use of the excerpt from Iyanla Vanzant's book *Until Today*. One of my favourite authors, this lady is truly inspirational.

PART 1

OUR ANCESTRAL INHERITANCE

To Dr. Ken McAll – Pioneer – A Dedication

The great modern day pioneer in the area of Family Tree Healing was the English Psychiatrist Ken McAll who died in 2004. His little book, 'Healing the Family Tree' first publisher in 1982, is still the most popular layman's guide on the subject and by providing keys to unlocking the mysteries of past generations has opened doors of freedom and healing for thousands. Born in China in 1910 he graduated in medicine from Edinburgh University. He returned to China as a missionary surgeon and was interned by the Japanese along with his wife and child for four years during the War. His experiences in China led him to have an interest in the powers of 'possession'. After returning to England he studied psychiatry and spent ten years in general practice followed by eighteen as a consultant psychiatrist.

Many patients referred to him during his consultancy years felt that they suffered from the presence of 'spirits' or the intrusion of voices from another realm which were audible only to themselves and which psychiatry dismissed as madness. After thorough medical examinations and with previous medical histories established, Dr. McAll came to the conclusion that in many cases these had a reality and that there was a distinction between them. Some seemed evil and could be traced to occult practices. Other seemed to be neutral, harmless voices begging for help. Occasionally the patient could identify the voice as belonging to a recently dead relative but often there was no known connection in the patient's mind.

Who were these unbidden and unquiet spirits and how could they hold people in bondage? After careful analysis of the person's personal and family history he felt he could hypothesize an answer, which he termed, 'possession syndrome'. According to this theory a passive, dependent person could so live their life through another person as to suffer the loss of their own identity and be unable to break free of the others control. As his work progressed McAll found it possible to classify the 'possession syndrome' into different categories and was able to make his diagnosis accordingly. These were:

1) The bondage of the living to the living.

2) The bondage of the living to the dead, whether to ancestors, to those not related, to stillborn or aborted babies or to those who once inhabited a particular place now occupied by the living.

3) The bondage of the living to occult control.

Back in the early eighties when my work in this area was just beginning to unfold Ken McAll came on a visit and, through our interaction and co-presenting some seminars, gave me the understanding and encouragement that I needed to continue. It was one of the most significant encounters of my life. To this great man of God, who in the time I was privileged to spend with him left indelible footprints in my heart, this book is dedicated.

Getting the Past out of the Present

The Ancestral Shadow

Cobra Vase

The piece illustrated is entitled the 'Cobra Vase', the cobra being one of the most dangerous reptiles. Each generation stands on the shoulders of the previous one. Much of what we inherit is of a positive nature, like looks, talents and personality traits. However we may find that we are not only being supported but also being poisoned by some aspect of our family history. It is as if our lives are being trespassed upon and there is a deep cry for forgiveness and resolution. This reality finds an echo in the Lord's Prayer 'forgive us our trespasses as we forgive those who trespass against us'.

Sometimes our connection with the past and those who have gone before us is painfully obvious, yet our eyes can be attuned to everything except the obvious. Jamie, a man in his early forties, was a top sportsman in his day until becoming almost crippled by chronic back trouble, to the extent of needing a wheelchair. With a little guidance he recognized a possible connection with his uncle who was also a top sportsman whom he was named after. This man had two children both of whom were drowned within days of each other. It was a tragedy he never got over. He became a violent alcoholic and died in misery. A very short time after his death Jamie's back trouble began for no apparent reason. After recognizing that his uncle may need prayer, Jamie again went to a physiotherapist and within minutes emerged a new man. The therapist remarked that it was the easiest job he ever had to perform, a simple manipulation procedure was all that was required to get the man back on his feet.

Jamie's story may sound remarkable, yet it is typical of so many who have recognized a direct link between their past family history and their own personal difficulties. John B. Keane's classic 'The Field' starring Richard Harris as the Bull McCabe struck a chord in the hearts of so many Irish with our strong affiliation to land. After watching the film and reflecting on his own family history one man remarked how his grandfather had got into a dispute with a neighbour over land. It was never resolved and he died full of bitterness. His Father also carried on the conflict and died an unhappy man. This man now felt that he had inherited not just the land but also the bitterness that was associated with it as well and unless he was prepared to forgive the injustice of an earlier generation, the resentment would not stop with him but would pass down into future generations as well.

As we progress into the 21st. century, Ancestral Healing, although a relatively new arrival on the therapeutic stage, is increasingly recognized as offering hope and providing insight into areas of suffering where previously there was none. It is also proving to be an effective means of healing addictions and physical and psychological problems that are passed down from one generation to another. Cancer, suicide and depression are all known to run in families, but so many other ailments like eating disorders, mood disorders, miscarriages, sexual problems, marital discord, infertility and early deaths, may well be linked to our invisible connections to the negative aspects of our ancestry.

Traumas and unhappiness don't just die with those who were the original victims; they remain to reverberate down through the family tree. Whether these echoes from the past manifest themselves as unhappy ghosts, physical illness or psychological problems, they can haunt us as descendants. In general it may be said that it is those traumas that have never been faced which tend to recur again and again. Alcoholism, mental illness, sexual abuse and suicide so often remain hidden, and as one generation sweeps them under the carpet, the next is left to pick up the pieces. So many of our problems can be older than ourselves, so how can we loosen the ties that bind us to the more negative aspects of our relatives' history to ensure that we face the future without the skeletons of the family closet rattling along behind us?

Ancestral Healing, also known as Healing the Family Tree, is an opportunity to recognize and bring healing to family influences from the past, in a way which has implications for the future. It suggests the possibility that negative acts and deeds of ancestors can somehow enter into our bloodstream or psyche and take a toll on future generations. Transforming the connection with these troublesome roots is what intergenerational healing is all about.

'To be ignorant of history is to be condemned to repeating it'

We are products of our past, both our own past, the family into which we were born, our ancestral history, and our country of origin. To the extent that we are unaware of our past, we are prisoners of it, and perhaps even condemned to repeating it as part of an on going pattern. In the words of an English poet who penned one of the shortest poems on record-

'History repeats itself,

Has to,

Nobody Listens'

The Swiss Psychiatrist Carl Jung's understanding of sin was that it was 'to remain in an unconscious state,' in other words to remain in a state of unawareness, refusing to face the truth of the past which may hold the key to our understanding of the present. Healing is about growth in awareness or making conscious that which was previously hidden. In the words of Christ 'You shall know the truth and the truth shall set you free'.

'Fateful' Issues

Carl Jung once said that unresolved personal issues, which we refuse to face and instead repress into our unconscious, would keep reappearing throughout our lives as 'Fate'. This we see in countless examples of where the outer circumstances of a person's life act as a tailor-made reflection of their inner reality. Could this not also be true in the intergenerational sense when we see particular families dogged by hardship, sickness, poverty and what is generally classed as 'bad luck', that this too is fate bearing a strong message? If this is true, then we must in some cases look to sources beyond the living to explain and resolve some of the problems of the living.

The past is never where we like to think we have left it.

Rather we carry it with us wherever we go.

Not a Panacea

Healing the Family Tree is just one aspect of the journey towards wholeness, and is not a panacea for all ills. It should never result in an abdication of personal responsibility, where all a person's psychological problems can now be blamed on past generations. It is much easier to blame than to take responsibility, especially where there are deep, painful issues arising from one's own life story, such as abuse, trauma or unresolved grief, which may take great courage to face. While it is unproductive to blame whatever has gone before, it is also detrimental to ignore the possible effects of past generations on present emotional conflicts.

Victim No More

For anyone desiring to bring healing to their family tree or who may be contemplating becoming involved in this area of healing, taking the reins or responsibility necessarily demands relinquishing the mentality of being a victim. Our outer reality is the creation of our inner reality whether that be personal or ancestral, conscious or unconscious. The way we see the outer world is always a mirror of our inner world.

The victim habitually sees himself or herself as being at the mercy of outside forces. Whether they are circumstances or people, these can always be blamed for that persons pitiable state. While in victim mode the person is always on the lookout for something or someone to blame, be that luck, fate, circumstances, ancestry, childhood, society, government, other people, church or even the weather. Blaming by its very nature gives away the very power we need to bring about change and so instead of assuming responsibility ourselves we abdicate it elsewhere.

There are other payoffs for being a victim apart from the avoidance of responsibility. Being magnets for disaster and continually in crisis victims tend to get a lot of love and attention. Others feel sorry and offer their sympathy vote. Clinging to the past makes it possible to indulge in lots of self-pity. They can feel very self-righteous and have excuses to inflict punishment on others. Perhaps this is why, on so many occasions before he performed a miracle, Christ asked the person who was afflicted, "Do you want to be made well?" The implication being that in becoming well one must take on the mantle of responsibility.

The avoidance of responsibility, which is so endemic, is presented in the Bible as being at the core of Original Sin. After Adam and Eve had eaten the forbidden fruit, God confronted them with what they had done. Adam immediately blamed both God and Eve saying, "It wasnít me Lord, it was that woman you put with me." When Eve was confronted she also sidestepped responsibility by pointing her finger at the serpent who of course hadnít a leg to stand on!

Jesus spoke of the broad road that so many follow and the narrow way that leads to life. The broad road could be considered the cul-de-sac of blame and the "narrow road that leads to life," as the path of responsibility. When I stop seeing myself as a victim I can then face the challenge of deciding, and being a co-creator, of what I really want my life to be.

Jesus' Family Tree

One of the big criticisms leveled by the Scribes and Pharisees against Jesus was that he was the friend of tax collectors and sinners. Why did these individuals who were ostracized by the religious people of the day feel so comfortable as to be able to frequent his company and want to share their table with him? Obviously they experienced Jesus as welcoming and totally non-judgmental. One explanation offered for this was that he might well have been aware of his own family tree and where he came from. A strong oral tradition probably existed at the time that gave children knowledge of their ancestral roots. Knowing whom he was, in the light of where he had come from, may well have helped him to embrace his mission of being sent in search of the sheep that were lost.

In the official genealogy of Jesus, tracing his Jewish ancestry back to Abraham there are numerous characters mentioned who had a dubious history. Among them, to name but a few, were Tamar, Rahab, Ruth, David and Bathsheba. Tamar seduced her father in order to get pregnant. Rahab was a prostitute. Ruth was a foreigner who broke the Jewish law by marrying a Jew. King David committed adultery with Bathsheba and then had her husband murdered. None of these would appear to be messianic material yet God brought good out of evil and Jesus came through their lineage. God's purpose is greater than our problems, our weaknesses, our failures or our sin. History ultimately is History. In the Divine economy all things are made to work together unto good. A master planner is at work incorporating even the most unlikely materials into the grand design. We are not the architects of great plans, as sometimes we like to think; rather, we are simply servants of a great architect.

Our Family Tree

A story is told of a family who hired a professional biographer in order to document the history of their family tree. One problem they were worried about was a certain Uncle George who had been executed in the electric chair having been convicted of murder. Voicing their concern to the biographer he could see no problem and came up with a creative solution. 'I will say that Uncle George occupied the chair of an important government institution. He was attached to his position by the strongest of ties, and his death came as a real shock.' Mark Twain once said that he spent a lot of money tracing his family tree, then twice as much trying to keep it a secret!

There is in human nature a very real tendency to reject, split off or disown any unacceptable elements that we discover either in ourselves as individuals or in our family history. This often takes the form of distorting the truth, as in the case of Uncle George, or in a deliberate attempt to air brush out of history events or individuals who do not fit into our idealized version of the way things should have been. This stands in marked contrast to the Biblical genealogy of Jesus that tells the story exactly as it is.

Uprooting Our Multi-Faceted Past

Root Sculpture

The piece shown is the root section of an oak tree that has been inverted. The picture was taken at its installation on a roundabout in Kilmore Quay. This is a tourist area with a busy port and marina, overlooking the world famous bird sanctuary of the Saltee Islands; the root branches are carved in a manner that expresses the different aspects of life in the area. So there are three fish, a gull in flight, the heads of three birds, two seals, a dog and a series of rocks. All the shoots are given character and definition both in the cleaning and carving process. In a graphic manner it reflects the process of uprooting and uncovering the various characters that are an integral part of our family tree.

As we embrace the fascinating world of uncovering our family tree we meet real people who were not much different in their thoughts and feelings to ourselves. We discover that we are all made of the same stuff but 'cooked' slightly differently because of living in a different milieu at a different time. In some cases they would have lived happy, fulfilled lives and died peacefully, while others would have died with feelings of guilt, anger, resentment, fear or remorse.

Whatever way we choose to look at it we are here because of them. Something of the complex tapestry of their lives is part of who we are. In our modern scientific age many find it absurd to think that the actions of an unknown ancestor could possibly have anything to do with them today. Yet in case after case it is often discovered that an individual's problems can be so much older than themselves and stretch back for several generations.

Benefits of Ancestral Healing

The benefits of engaging in ancestral healing are enormous:

• To know where we have come from is essential to knowing who we are and where we are going.

• We release the positive gifts that are part of our ancestry.

• Behavioral patterns in ourselves can be understood differently.

• Once old destructive patterns have been identified we can make new and positive choices.

• By healing the past we also free up conditions for the future.

• Physical conditions stemming from our forbearers can be healed.

• We regain our sense of wonder and awe at the mystery of life.

Sin – A Biblical Perspective

Measuring Up

The piece shown is a target disk with concentric rings. On either side is a measuring tape and an ornate cup. These are made from sycamore, purple heart and ebony. They are set into a piece of darkened burr elm with an oak base. In a symbolic manner it represents different aspects of the Christian message on sin and redemption.

The word 'sin' as used in the Bible comes from the Greek word *'hamartia'*. This is taken from the art of archery and literally means 'to miss the mark'. From this we can extrapolate that sin is the state of being aimless, goalless or lacking vision. Christian teaching states quite clearly that all have sinned or failed to measure up. We have missed the mark and fallen short of the glory of God. (Rom. 3:23) It is through faith in Christ and in the Cup of Salvation that he offers that we are justified (just as if I had never sinned) and united with God.

In Baptism we become God's adopted sons through Christ (Ephs. 1:5). If it is the case that in Christ our sin is forgiven and we are made righteous then how can we explain Purgatory? The reality is:

• Many die unrepentant and not in right relationship with Christ.

• Many die with resentment and unforgiveness towards others.

• Many die lacking forgiveness towards themselves.

• Many die unprepared and with unfinished business.

• Many die as they have lived, totally ego-centered.

• Many die with unresolved hurts and buried issues.

• Many die never having lived, their lives always governed by fear.

• Many die but are still too attached to this world to move on.

• Many die but are held onto by others in morbid grief.

• Many die in denial and must face the hurt they have caused others.

Praying for the Deceased

The Christian practice of praying for the dead is steeped in tradition with its roots stretching deep into the Old Testament. One example from 2 Maccabees 12:45 states that, 'It is a holy and pious thought to pray for the dead that they might be freed from their sins'.

The lives of the saints from the early Church abound with examples of those who helped the dead by their prayers. One example was St. Perpetua who died in 203A.D. While she was in prison, her dead and unbaptised brother, Dinocrates, appeared to her in a vision. He appeared to be wounded, pale, thirsty and unable to drink from a fountain. After several days praying for him to be taken up unto Heaven, she was rewarded with a vision of him happy, healed and able to drink from the eternal fountain.

Many traditions other than Roman Catholic hold to the practice of praying for the dead. The Eastern Orthodox believes in the power of prayer to help even those in Hell which contrary to the Catholic view is not understood as a place of permanence. Some Methodists are returning to the tradition of John Wesley who encouraged his flock to pray for the faithful departed. He was steeped in the Anglican tradition, which today is rediscovering that prayer for the deceased is as traditional as The Book Of Common Prayer. A group of Anglican theologians reporting to the 'Archbishop's Commission on Christian Doctrine' wrote of how the living may usefully pray for the dead that during their state of purification they may develop, 'A deepening of character and a greater maturity of personality.'

Carl Jung himself came from a strong Protestant background and in his work 'Psychology and Religion' he states his view that, 'Mourners should not build huge funeral monuments but should rather pray for their dead as Catholics do at the Eucharist.'

It is a central belief in Catholicism that for many of the departed there may be an intermediate stage between earth and Heaven called Purgatory. It is generally understood as a state, and not necessarily a place, of purification. This belief finds expression in having prayers and Masses offered for the dead. The month of November especially is associated with being a time of remembrance for the faithful departed with particular emphasis on Nov. 2nd as All Souls Day. Generation after generation of Catholics has prayed fervently for the suffering souls in Purgatory as an essential part of their faith practice.

Clinical Death Experiences

Contemporary research with resuscitated patients who report their experience of clinical death also support the belief that some of the deceased may need the prayers of the living in order to continue their journey on the other side. A pioneer in this area is Dr. Raymond Moody. His research suggests that there seems to be a period of adjustment after death for, 'learning and receiving correction.' Many patients report seeing, 'a realm of dejected spirits' in which the dead are trapped and are trying to communicate with their living relatives in the hope of moving on to Heaven. Some said that it looked as if their God was down here; others felt that souls in that realm appeared to be either holding onto someone or something on earth or were in fact being held onto by people in this earthly realm. Could it be that clinging onto someone in morbid grief or resentment can hold a person bound on the other side? After all we cannot be identified merely with our bodies, so is it not reasonable to suppose that whatever has the power to bind us on this side can also affect us on the other side?

Letting Go

From the island of Crete comes this beautiful story:

An old man loved his native island with a deep and passionate love. As he lay dying he had his sons bring him outside and lay him on his beloved earth. As he was about to expire, he reached down by his side and clasped some earth into his hands.

At Heaven's gate, God as an old white haired man came out to greet him and welcome him into the joys of Heaven. As he started to enter the pearly gates God said, 'Please you must let the soil go, only those with open hands can receive the kingdom.' Never! Never!' said the old man, stepping back, 'Never!' And so God departed sadly, leaving him outside the gates.

A few eons went by and God came out again, this time as a friend and old drinking crony. They had a few drinks, told a few stories and then God said, 'Now friend its time to enter heaven, so lets go.' Once again he requested that the man let go of the soil and once more he refused.

More eons rolled by and God appeared again, this time as a delightful granddaughter. 'Granddad,' she said, 'you're so wonderful and we all miss you, please come inside with me.' The old man nodded and she went to help him up for by this time he had grown very old and feeble. They moved towards the pearly gates and at this point his strength gave out. He reached out to save himself and his gnarled fingers could no longer stay clenched in a fist with the result that the soil sifted out between them until his hands were empty. So he was free to enter Heaven. What was the first sight that greeted him? His beloved Island of Crete.

Working with the Dying

Pastoral practice of working with those preparing for death affirms the need for the soul to be helped to let go of whatever might be weighing it down before it can continue its journey. One of the first experiences that shaped my understanding in this area happened while I was still in seminary. It concerned a woman in her forties who was dying of cancer in a Dublin hospital. Very late one night I felt an urgent need to pray for her. For a while I experienced a great sense of struggle and turmoil that eventually gave way to peace. At this stage I went to sleep and thought no more about it until the following evening when I went to visit her. She asked if I knew what had happened the previous night? I replied that I wasn't sure and invited her to tell me. 'I died', she said, 'and as my soul left my body I got an awful shock to see how small my body had become, but I didn't go to Heaven. Instead I got stuck somewhere between light and darkness and there seemed to be forces pulling at me from both sides. I knew that I was in trouble and cried for help. Then I felt something happening, and as I looked down I saw you praying and I could feel its effect drawing me back into my body. I knew then that I had been saved from something dreadful.'

Listening to her account, I sensed that there had to be a very good reason as to why darkness should have such a hold over her, so I gently probed as to what it might be. She went on to reveal something that was hugely significant in her life that she had never spoken to anyone about and had not come to terms with. This was the key to unblocking her spirit and some hours later she died in wonderful peace. I can still recall such a deep sense of joy permeating her funeral that it even transcended the sadness of her passing.

The Lights Of Heaven

An elderly man was dying in hospital. The chaplain had been around and given him the last rites. 'Officially' he was prepared for the journey. At another level he was deeply distressed and agitated. Passing close to the bed his mental anguish drew my attention. After a brief conversation, where he told me that he knew he was dying, I led him in a prayer of surrender of his life to the Lord. At a certain point he was unable to continue. I felt drawn to ask him if there was anyone that he needed to forgive. 'Yes', he said, 'my brother and sister; we haven't spoken for forty years; the hurt has been killing me.' With his life ebbing away it was far too late to make contact with his relatives. I encouraged him to forgive them from his heart and to release the hurt to the Lord. Almost immediately his eyes took on a far away look so I asked him what he was seeing. He smiled peacefully and said, 'The Lights of Heaven; how absolutely lovely.' Shortly afterwards he passed away. It was a chance encounter and I wondered what fate was awaiting him had he continued to allow resentment to keep him bound.

Unhealed Grief

An old nun of ninety-five had been seriously ill and trying to die for six months. She hadn't eaten for ages and something appeared to be holding her back. While praying with her I felt drawn to ask about her relationship with her mother. She told me that her mother had died when she was five and then she began to cry. It seemed to be the tears more of a five year old who was grieving her mum than those of a ninety-five year old. As I helped her to hand her mother over to the Lord she found great peace. Just hours later she passed away after apparently having found the freedom to do so. Other sisters in the convent remarked that even though she was a lovely person she had had a miserable life. She had always carried a burden that prevented her from finding peace and happiness.

The above story is just one of many where holding onto someone in unresolved grief prevents a person from letting go in death and being poor enough in spirit to receive the kingdom with open hands.

A Dream Connection

At a workshop on dreams a young woman shared one example of many beautiful dreams she had regarding her father. In the dream he was kind, supportive, encouraging and everything a good father should be. She went on to say how her dreams had changed about him over a number of years. In life he had been a serious alcoholic who had treated his family badly and often left them short. Because of his drink problem she felt that she never really knew him. After his untimely death her dreams about him were quite scary. He sometimes appeared to be in darkness and in others very confused. At some point he appeared to be asking for her forgiveness. This didn't happen for about a year as she struggled to come to terms with his legacy of hurt. Eventually her decision was made; she began to pray for him and had Masses offered. Almost immediately her dreams changed dramatically and she seemed to be seeing the man she never knew, the real person who had always been buried beneath his problems. Since then she looked forward to meeting her father in her dreams and felt that in death she now had a far closer relationship with him than when he was alive.

Connections with Ancestry

What We Inherit

Three Chinese Balls

The piece shown is a set of Chinese Balls. It comprises three spheres, one inside the other. Each carries the same pattern as the outer sphere from which they were created. The ancient art of being able to create spheres from within spheres is a source of fascination for those who see them. Perhaps of all the mysterious objects produced by the oriental craftsman, Chinese Balls have retained their sense of mystery the longest. They also provide a useful symbol for the mysterious connection between the various generations.

We are products not just of our own history but also of our ancestry. As we trace our individual problems we often find that what we are experiencing is part of a pattern that has been recurring through several generations. We may come to understand that we are not just products of ancestry but also prisoners of it as well. There are ties which bind us to the more negative aspects of our relatives' history and recognizing this we realize that our problems can sometimes be much older than ourselves.

Pulling Strings

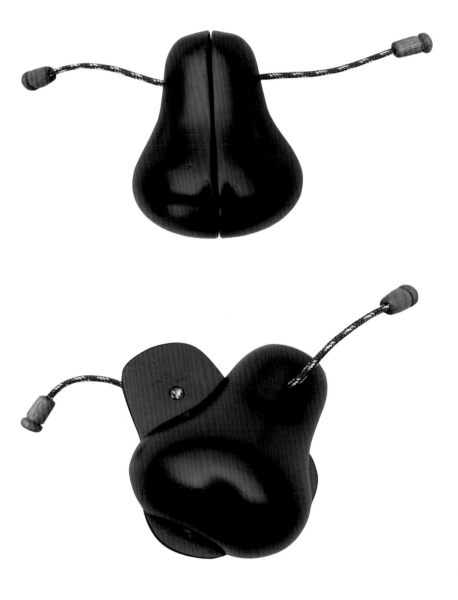

A Puzzling Pear

The split pear puzzle provides a powerful illustration of what happens when we attempt to cut off or disassociate from parts of our reality. The string at the top of the pear is seen to be passing through a hole connecting both halves. If the string is pulled on one side the other is pulled inwards and vise versa. A sharp knife is inserted in the gap and the string cut in two. The two halves can then be twisted apart and the cut ends revealed as in the second photograph. Next the two halves are put back into shape and when the cord is pulled it is found to be working exactly as before. It is as if a magical 're-pear' has been achieved.

Disowning our Dark Side

There is a universal tendency in human nature to cut, split off or separate from painful or shameful experiences and lock the door on them in the mistaken belief that if ignored they will go away. At a personal level we may think that we have cut ourselves free from aspects of our past only to experience that it still exercises a mysterious pull over our lives. Leaving home is to separate from our parents but we still carry their influence wherever we go. We may split off what we deem to be unacceptable emotions only to find that they keep returning to haunt us. When a relationship becomes too difficult or complicated we may resort to using the scissors treatment and think that by cutting that person out of our lives and having nothing more to do with them that the problem is solved. Usually we discover, much to our surprise, that he or she still has the power to pull our strings and control our thoughts just as much as ever.

Where an entire family is affected by some traumatic event, such as a suicide, a member going insane, a grave injustice or a violent death, there is a strong likelihood that instead of the issue being addressed and resolved in a healthy way it will be cut off, put underground, not spoken about and 'buried alive'. As a result many families have 'skeletons' carefully locked away but still very much alive in so far as they are unresolved and unreconciled. A man and his wife once ordered a very large wardrobe for their bedroom. The carpenter expressed doubts that one of such size could be got through the door and asked if they really needed it to be quite so big? 'Certainly we do', the man replied. 'You have no idea the size of the skeletons we have in our family!' Another such story relates to an American who returned to Ireland to find out about his family tree. He was told that no such information would be forthcoming since his branch had been cut off!

Just as personal issues, which are cut off, tend to recur again and again, so also is the case with ancestral issues where a legacy of unfinished business from one generation passes down to another.

The Blame Game

In Liverpoolís National Museum there is a famous painting by William Holman Hunt (1827-1910) entitled 'The Scapegoat'. The only figure in the picture is a disheveled and solitary goat. It was a painting that met with a cool and dismissive response from the critics who first saw it. What they did not know was that it came as the result of years of intense study of the Talmud, particularly Leviticus 16, in its geographical setting. During his time in the Holy Land Hunt was gripped by the significance of the annual ritual at the Jewish Festival of Atonement (Yom Kippur) during which the sins of the people, their faults and all their transgressions and all their sins were laid on the head of a designated goat who was then driven from the temple into the wilderness of Edom branded with scarlet on its head as a badge of shame. Banished into the desert, goaded to certain starvation and death, the scapegoat shouldered all that was blameworthy in the community. The people were then "free", their guilt expunged and they could feel clean again.

The ancient Leviticus text is still acutely relevant in terms of the kind of people that we are how far we are prepared to go in the lurid business of shifting the blame and projecting our shadow onto someone else. We may abhor the idea of being cruel to a goat yet naming, blaming and shaming "that other" while keeping our own house clean is endemic in families and society at large.

It is not uncommon for family genograms to reveal that in almost every generation there is a scapegoat; a troubled, burdened and rejected member who is unconsciously carrying the dark side of what might appear to be a very upright, respectable and religious family. Usually the brighter and more successful that family appears to the world the more intensely their shadow side is constellated and projected onto some unfortunate member. That persons plight often drives then out into the wilderness of alcoholism or other addictions and after a life marked by tragedy they so often die utterly alone, unloved and unmourned.

A Victim Perspective

The following story represents just one scenario of how someone can be cast into the scapegoat role. Mary Rose was a typical scapegoat who all her life had felt that she was the black sheep in her family. She was the eldest girl from a father and mother who were very divided. A close but unhealthy bond developed between herself and her father and from an early age he abused her sexually. Her mother deeply resented this "special" relationship and blamed Mary Rose for everything that was going wrong. Many years later, even when this man was convicted for sexual abuse, she was overheard saying that everything that happened was all her daughterís fault. The other siblings also resented the bond between Mary Rose and her father and so they dumped their anger onto her as well.

In describing herself as a scapegoat Mary Roses expresses what is the reality for so many in her unenviable position.

• Carrying a huge level of responsibility.

• Feeling trapped and burdened.

• Weighed down by guilt and shame.

• Always being blamed and blaming herself.

• Taking everything as deserved punishment.

• Driven to distraction and despair.

• Never able to get it right with the family.

• Being the outsider yet stuck in the middle of chaos.

• Being rejected and not allowed to belong.

• Having an overwhelming sadness and despondency.

• Caught in spiders web with the more struggle the more enmeshment.

• Coming home is like being sucked into a dark hole of negative energy.

Being able to identify the dynamics of what is taking place can be a big help for the victim because in the absence of naming the problem it is difficult to find a solution. The scapegoat is burdened by family shame but over years has displaced that shame onto himself or herself. Learning to disidentify from family projections is also crucial to recovery. Carrying guilt and shame also erodes self-esteem so part of the healing process must involve restructuring ones personal beliefs and adopting a totally positive view of Self.

No-One is an Island

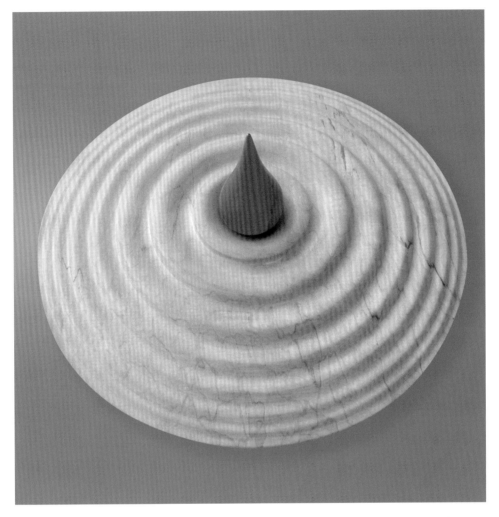

A Drop In the Ocean

The piece entitled *A Drop in the Ocean* could just as well be called *Influence*. Long after the drop has fallen and become one with the ocean the ripples still fan out. No-one's life exists in isolation from others, and how we choose to live our lives continues to have its influence whether for good or bad.

The most familiar scriptural reference to this phenomenon is from Exodus 20:5 where it speaks of the sins of the fathers being visited on the children. This concept is one that many find very hard to understand. How could a just and loving God punish one generation for the sins of another?

Initially, this was viewed by the Jews in the context of the extended family, perhaps all living under the one roof. The great-grandfather could see in no uncertain terms that how he had lived out his years in fidelity to Yahweh, had a direct bearing on all the succeeding generations, down to the smallest toddler in the household. The life and death of each of us has its influence on others, for good or for bad. Another interesting verse that carries this important truth comes from the Prophet Ezekiel, where he quotes a saying that was popular in his time, 'The fathers have eaten sour grapes and the children's teeth are set on edge'.

There is an ever growing body of people who perhaps having attended counsellors for years, have experienced little progress and felt 'stuck' at the personal level. Yet when a deeper investigation into the family history is undertaken, and the relevant truth unearthed, an entirely new freedom emerges and unprecedented progress is made on the inner journey.

Generational Cover Up

John was a professional man who was heavily burdened most of his life. His family only saw him free of this for a brief period of three years and that was while his only son was dying of an incurable disease. After the son's death he immediately returned to his normal depressed state where he remained until he took his life at eighty-two. In the months that followed, his eldest daughter felt that whatever had been weighing down her father all his life had now passed to her. Now this woman who had never known a day's depression could barely lift her head. The family history revealed that in a previous generation there had been a major cover up of a family secret, where a girl had been totally rejected because of getting pregnant, and all her subsequent family had been ostracized as well. This truth had been so well hidden that it was only uncovered after considerable effort. As part of a healing ritual a number of family members went to visit the graves of those who had suffered such injustice and, in the context of a Eucharist, offered an apology on behalf of those who were originally responsible. This turned out to be the key to restoring the woman to her normal sense of well-being.

A Mother's Legacy of Grief

Jonathan was a successful property developer who in a few short years made lots of money and was very involved in public life. He enjoyed a happy marriage but always said that he never felt well since the time he got married. This was also the time that his mother died after three years of serious illness and his father died some months later. A number of years after getting married Jonathan's wife developed health problems which were a cause for concern and this, together with overwork, triggered him into having a nervous breakdown. For the next six years his life was spent in and out of psychiatric care and eventually he was put on the strongest possible dose of medication. This meant that while he had an existence, he was totally lacking a life. Jonathan's problems could be traced back to his mother's death. While they were extremely close, her demise in itself was not enough to create such a profound psychic disturbance. It was what his mother was carrying up to the day she died which transferred to him as a kind of legacy that proved to be the key factor in ensuring Jonathan's release. Brutalized as a child by her family, she fell deeply in love and married the man of her dreams. When six months pregnant with her first child, her husband was killed in a terrible accident. She bore a son whom she idolized, and probably substituted for his dead father. As a young man he committed suicide which was the ultimate heartbreak for a woman who had already suffered so much. Jonathan was the son of her second marriage to a man she never could love as much as her first. He became extra special and unconsciously was filling the void left in his mother's heart by the loss of the two most significant men in her life. At a deeper level he was no doubt being identified with both of these individuals whose lives had been marked by tragedy. This only came to its culmination after his mother died, and so it was from there on that he always felt burdened and unwell. After that time he was not just dealing with his grief over her death but was also now a bearer of her intolerable grief and hardship.

A Legacy of Coldness

Tracy remarked in casual conversation that she had severed all emotional ties with her family at six years of age. With a little encouragement the pattern of cutting emotional ties began slowly to become clear. Her great-grandmother had six children. Her husband was drowned at sea and around that time diphtheria swept through the Isle of Man where they were living. This eventually claimed the lives of five of her children. Years later she remarried and had one more child whom she never encouraged to have any emotional connection with her firstborn who was the survivor. In severing her emotional connection with her past, she also excluded her own child who was the living reminder of that terrible past. That child grew up to become Tracy's mother and now the grandmother's legacy was ready to be passed down to another generation.

A Forced Adoption

A seminar on Family Tree Healing concluded with a celebration of the Eucharist on the Sunday afternoon. There a woman apologized on behalf of her deceased parents for forcing her sister to have her child adopted. This happened when the girl was eighteen and it was something from which she had never recovered. A few days later a letter was received from the adopted girl seeking to make contact with her natural mother. The letter had been written on the Sunday evening shortly after the Mass!

The Mass and The Poor Souls

There is an interesting story from the Irish tradition that captures the ancient belief about the poor souls and the importance of the Mass. It was told on many occasions by Eamon Kelly, the well-known Irish actor and prince of storytellers.

It concerns a lost soul that was in total darkness and clinging to the back of an ivy leaf. There was no sound ever in the dark except perhaps an ivy leaf flapping in the wind. One time the soul heard someone laughing and said: 'Who is that?' And wasn't it another soul at the other side of the ivy leaf. 'How long have you been there?' says the first soul, and the second one said, 'Three times three score years.' 'I'm here longer than that,' the first soul said, 'I've lost all track of time, but tell me why were you laughing there now?' 'Because I heard good news,' the second soul said. 'Just now wasn't there a son born to the son of my son's great-grandson, and when he's twenty four-years of age he'll be ordained. At his first Mass he'll remember all those of his own family gone before him and that morning I'll be free! Did you hear me?' he said, for the first soul didn't answer. 'I did,' he said, 'fine for you. I've no one belonging to me.' 'Have courage,' the second soul said. 'Do you know what I'll do? Whatever good is coming from that Mass I'll go halves in that with you!'

In typical story telling fashion Eamon concludes the story with, 'Our Lord and his mother went out for a walk and happened to overhear the conversation. So she says to him. ' Did you hear that?' He said, 'I did, what about it?' 'To think,' she said, ' that that lost soul after waited so long for his freedom, and then when the means of his release comes he's willing to share it with a complete stranger. What are you going to do about it?' 'Well, I suppose' says He, 'I'll have to do something!' She went away and put the sheets airing, and that night St. Peter was asked to send a special invite to the two lost souls that had just been found!

Generational Trauma

Past Events and Present Realities

Ingrained Trauma

Post Traumatic Stress Disorder can be defined as the condition whereby a person, or family, or community, survives a traumatic event, but still suffers the psychological effects. While considerable time may have elapsed since the actual event, a part of the emotional life has been left behind, and this creates a host of symptoms, which are almost invariably blamed on something else. Up to recent years when soldiers returned from war, many were so traumatized by what they had been through that they suffered from this condition. Because it was not understood, it went untreated, and they were classed as being 'shell shocked'. A welcome development, in recent times, is the recognition of the need to have counselling available both to survivors, rescuers and families who have been involved in life threatening situations. Even with an ever-deepening awareness of this condition, it is still widespread, and vast numbers of people have a life that only amounts to an existence because of it.

Trauma – How not to Respond!

There's an elephant in the room
It is large and squatting, so it's hard to get around it.
Yet we squeeze by with, 'How are you' and 'I'm fine,'
And a thousand other forms of trivial chatter.
We talk about the weather.
We talk about work.
We talk about everything –
Except the elephant in the living room.

There's an elephant in the room.
We all know it is there.
We are thinking about the elephant as we talk together.
It is constantly on our minds.
For you see it is a very big elephant.
It has hurt us all.
But we do not talk about the elephant in the room.

Please talk about the elephant,
Because if you don't you are forcing me into isolation
Into being left alone in a room
With an elephant.

The story of the elephant in the living room provides a useful backdrop for understanding how a traumatic event that happens in a family can affect the people involved and permeate down into subsequent generations when it is not spoken about or acknowledged. Trauma by its very nature demands total acknowledgement by the people most immediately affected. Without this healing cannot take place. Where the event is not spoken about, like the elephant, it sinks deeper and deeper into the unconscious where it begins to fester and eventually affects everyone in the family. With each subsequent generation the trauma becomes more distant in time and its effects become more deeply embedded in the form of an emotional memory. Present events can awaken these earlier memories and colour our perceptions of them. For instance a grave injustice can be awakened by a minor offence causing the offended party to make a disproportionate response. It is the original trauma that is being reacted to, but without an awareness of this happening a solution to the present difficulty will be difficult to find. Many court settlements leave a bitter taste in people's mouths because what appears to be the real issue of contention isn't the real issue at all. The settlement that is really required is of a much earlier nature.

At another level if we take on board the principle that inner realities create outer events, then the circumstances of the original trauma will be replicated in different forms through each generation. Hence many families find themselves in a vicious cycle of recycled traumas.

Invisible Loyalties

Since the condition of Post Traumatic Stress Disorder has been identified, it has been applied primarily to individuals as isolated entities. There is now a growing awareness that trauma often exists in the consciousness of families, communities and cultures in a manner that transcends any one generation. The relatively new field of Transgenerational Psychotherapy deals with events and behaviour patterns that can be traced back through several generations with the intention of discovering the original trauma that was responsible for those patterns.

The basic theory of Transgenerational Psychotherapy is that when a trauma remains unresolved and unhealed in one generation it has the capacity to generate an ongoing behaviour pattern that appears in each succeeding generation. This then becomes a family trait. For example a particular family who are characterized by their greed for land may have a history of being evicted from their land in an earlier generation. At an unconscious level a dynamic is at work trying to balance the accounts and regain what was taken at an earlier time. Similarly a very materialistic family who buy strongly into the myth that to have more means to be more may be reacting to a period of their family history where they were made to feel worthless because of their poverty.

Issues and Tissues

As well as behaviour patterns being passed down many physical conditions resulting from the original trauma can pass into succeeding generations. Family Tree Ministry provides much evidence to suggest that unresolved issues both at a personal and ancestral level can become somatised and many families have genetic conditions which characterize them resulting from earlier events which have never been recognized. In one case four generations of eldest sons were known to have suffered from abdominal pain. The family history revealed a great injustice had been done to an ancestor who handed over his farm to his eldest son on the understanding that he would be cared for in his old age. Instead he was ousted from his home and died destitute, probably with great bitterness. From there on the eldest in the family suffered in a physical manner the echoes this man's emotional trauma. As happens in these kind of cases when the pain suffered by this wounded individual was acknowledged and a family member apologized on behalf of his forbearers for what had happened the complaints of the remaining two eldest disappeared and never occurred again.

Issues and Attitudes

Transgenerational Psychotherapy also recognizes that attitudes associated with the original trauma can become the legacy of future generations. Usually these are handed down without question and create automatic attitudes and behaviour in situations that mimic the original trauma. In effect the original trauma is kept alive through these responses. Such was the case of a family who over seventy years ago had a member who was caught red-handed while breaking and entering. It was believed that excessive force was used to arrest the man and he died in custody from injuries sustained. No enquiry was made and no apology issued. This became a festering wound in subsequent generations and each time a scab would form it would just as quickly be torn away whenever any member had a brush with the law. The anger released at the Gardai while simply doing their duty would often lead to an arrest and so the cycle continues and will continue until the original hurt is dealt with.

In his book *The Ancestor Syndrome* Schutzenberger says of cases like the above that, *'Fidelity to ancestors which has become unconscious and invisible governs us. It is important to make it visible, to become aware of it, to understand what impels us, and possibly to see if we may not have to reframe this loyalty in order to become free again to live our own lives.'*

Again, taking the war in Kosovo as an example, at the social level he pinpoints the dates of a series of battles between the Muslim Turks and the Serb Christians representing an injustice to one side or the other through several generations showing a remarkable similarity between the dates. The injustice behind one battle leads to a cycle of revenge leading to the next battle generations later. In relation to this and in particular to family dynamics he says:

'There is implicit family bookkeeping and some people cannot manage to forgive injustices which have been suffered. When family ledgers are not balanced, problems can be passed on from generation to generation. We pay the debt of earlier generations through this invisible loyalty.'

Reactions as Clues

It takes a considerable degree of maturity to recognize that our reactions are uniquely our own and don't provide an accurate indicator as to the truth of a given situation. What make one person angry or sad or fearful may elicit an entirely different response in someone else. The degree of stress we experience in different situations varies from person to person because ultimately it is not the situation that upsets us but rather it is we who are upset by the situation. It is never an accident that similar kinds of situations always trigger the same stressful response or indeed that the same kinds of stressful situations seem to appear over and over in our lives. Hence it is a rewarding exercise to continually monitor our reactions and recognize the situations that always make us feel in a particular way. From doing this we may gain valuable insight into our own individual story and often into our family history. It is always worth remembering that our response to any situation is always based on our own previous experiences and on our own family background, usually when we are not consciously aware of them. The causes of stress are the hidden and unresolved traumatic events that are triggered by circumstances that in some measure mirror the original event.

Where a trauma, whether personal or familial, is activated through an event of a similar nature, the individual often finds himself at lightening speed regressing into a time warp. Here he seems to have little or no choice but to think or act as he did or as his ancestor did in the original situation. The behaviour takes on an automatic nature. In effect this means that the person is reliving the original event instead of living with and relating to the current one.

Integration and Healing

Cradling the Rose

The rose is something we associate with being a thing of beauty, and yet it is very fragile. The picture of the hands, gently supporting the rose, is a fitting symbol of that part of the delicate emotional life which has been traumatized, and needs to be recognized and caressed back into life. The word **CRAB** provides a useful acronym for this healing process.

Choose to fix the problem rather than fix the blame on whoever activated the emotions. It is never possible to do both at the same time.

Recognize how these emotions have a personalized 'ring tone' l ike that found on some mobile phones. You will have heard from them before.

Accept them when they come knocking on your door. Rather than turn them away, treat them like welcome guests who may be bearing precious gifts from far away places.

Befriend the emotions, no matter how uncomfortable they feel or how negative they appear. This is the key that brings about integration and unlocks their transforming potential.

Requirements

What do our Ancestors need from us?

After many years of working with ancestral patterns there would appear to be three main responses that our ancestors require from us. These are:

- **Acknowledgement**
- **Understanding**
- **Forgiveness**

The Embrace

Crafted to reflect the Everlasting Arms and the Divine Embrace the above piece also contains in its essence the above three qualities.

Acknowledgement

We are who we are and we owe our very existence to those who went before us, yet surprisingly many of these may never have been acknowledged. There may even have been deliberate attempts made to air brush them out of the family tree. In some cases their names were never recorded even on a headstone; it was as if they never existed. Not surprisingly therefore a basic need for some ancestors is simple acknowledgement. A soldier could have been forced to go to war for economic reasons. When he went missing in action fighting for the British this became a matter of shame for his Republican family who never spoke about him again. Such was the case of many Irish soldiers who fought and died in the First World War. Where a parent or grandparent was illegitimate it would have been common practice for the father's name not to be recorded on the birth certificate. Even where the name is not available a prayerful acknowledgement and thanks for the gift of life may be quite appropriate.

Many individuals report feeling an enormous sense of relief and sometimes surprise when contact is first re-established with the ancestor. It is as though they have been waiting, sometimes very impatiently, for recognition before they can move on. Occasionally it may be possible to give that acknowledgement a practical dimension, like visiting their grave or having their name inscribed on a memorial. Many others find that remembering the ancestor and bringing him/her into normal conversation greatly improves the quality of relationships between the living members and releases a lot of blocked energy making communication a lot easier.

Understanding

The preface of the Church's Eucharistic Prayer on Reconciliation says: 'Your Spirit is at work when understanding puts an end to strife and vengeance gives way to forgiveness'. Understanding paves the way for forgiveness and is necessary for it. The more we seek understanding the less we are inclined to be judgmental or vengeful and the easier we find it to forgive. A girl who disgraced the family may have been the victim of abuse or rape. She may have attempted to tell her story and not been heard. A black sheep who died an alcoholic may have been scapegoated by his family who blamed everything on him and refused to take any responsibility for their own conduct. The social and economic climate of their lives may have driven some to take desperate measures that led other family members to disown them. An attempt to understand their story may make us realize that under similar circumstances we might have acted no differently to them. The search for underlying causes in the behaviour of our ancestors often gives us valuable insight into similar drives within ourselves.

John was named after his grandfather who was a First World War veteran. This man was badly wounded and during recovery fell deeply in love with the nurse who was looking after him. This romance blossomed but never materialized into marriage because of the circumstances of war. Instead he married someone else, a woman whom he respected but never loved. An obvious victim of Post

Traumatic Stress he was a very angry man who controlled his family with an iron fist. His eldest son grew up to be very aggressive and for the slightest provocation lost his temper. Because of him being so hard to live with the problem spilled over into the next generation and his son had major difficulties relating to his father while growing up. He too developed a short fuse and tended to resort to violence all to easily. Reflecting on his grandfather, to whom he was so often likened, John came to understand the origins of the anger that was so deeply buried within himself. His relationship with his father immediately improved, he no longer expected him to change and they became good friends. Similarly his own anger that had been problematic for so long became a wonderful creative force in his life.

Forgiveness

The Crossroads of Forgiveness

Forgiveness is represented as a crossroads with the centre pillar as the present, and the other two signposts as past and future. It is significant that the sign representing the past is made mostly from the darker wood and points downwards. Forgiveness can be understood as a moment in the present, which releases us from darkness of the past and opens up a bright new future.

Forgiveness is the key to freedom both for the dead and the living. It is defined in dictionaries as giving up resentment and abandoning all claims against a debtor. Often guilt over some foul deed, or resentment for some act, is a legacy that can be passed from generation to generation. In most cases those in the present are only aware that they struggle with feelings of guilt, unworthiness or resentment without any understanding as to where it may have originated. A family member who committed a murder may well leave such a legacy of guilt while an eviction or any other form of dispossession may leave a legacy of resentment. Many Irish people, because of our political history, struggle with such feelings giving rise to the term 'Irish Alzheimer's', where we forget everything except the grudge! It is not uncommon for someone to die feeling that the deed they committed was beyond forgiveness because it was just too big. Those who came after him may have shared such a limited understanding of God's mercy and believed that they too were outside the pale of divine love.

One such case history involved a man who lived in the Cork area. He was a wealthy, well-to-do landlord, married with no children, but having an affair. He decided to murder his wife and pin the blame on the servant girl who worked in the home. He successfully concocted a plot where the murder appeared to have been committed while he was at church and only the girl was at home with his wife. The girl was subsequently convicted and spent the rest of her life in the local mental institution. It was only on his deathbed, when that unfortunate woman had spent over fifty years in the asylum, that he confessed to what he had done. It is highly unlikely that he died having forgiven himself and so his children, born to his second wife, were forced to grapple with the issue of guilt and forgiveness for a long time afterwards. The awareness of their father's actions undermined the very foundations of their existence. Eventually it became absolutely necessary to forgive him in order to set themselves free and to offer a sincere apology to the Lord for the terrible injustice that he had committed. The victim of the injustice was still alive and as one gesture of restitution was able to end her days in one of the finest nursing homes available.

Suicide and The Beyond

Remembrance Vase

Since suicide is never a positive option, it has long been held that it may impede the spirit's progress on the other side. Inevitably with someone taking their own life there is a greater degree of unfinished business and the grieving process is more complicated than in the case of a normal death.

In the past the church taught that suicide was a mortal sin and even refused to allow victims to be buried in consecrated ground. Today, while the act is still considered to be objectively wrong, there is much more compassion and understanding for the person who was driven to take such desperate measures.

Many spiritually minded people would hold the view that if someone attempts suicide but fails, what they most need is help rather than judgment and thankfully this is what is usually offered. If that is true on this side, surely it must be similar, and even more so, on the other side. Is healing and understanding not available there also enabling them to understand the causes of their actions and come to terms with their lives?

The numerous clinical death accounts of those who were resuscitated after attempting to take their own lives sheds some significant light on this important subject. From their brief vantage point on the other side they express viewpoints that are remarkably similar. The following is a brief synopsis:

It is they themselves who must consider whether or not their actions were justified. To have jumped from high-rise building, as in the case of the Twin Towers on 9/11, is an objective act of self-destruction but subjectively very brave and justifiable. This analogy may also be applied to someone suffering from a mental illness where the inner torment has become unbearable and all other options have been exhausted.

Any suffering that is experienced comes as a result of self-recrimination and not because they are being punished. The awareness of the suffering they have caused to loved ones and having wasted their God-given opportunities is one of the major causes of suffering.

Some are acutely aware that they have left behind a legacy of anger and unforgiveness that will make it difficult for them and for their families to move on. One of the big regrets is not being able to say sorry to loved ones for the suffering they have caused. Others express the view that loved ones may continue to hold onto them in morbid grief and that this will impede their progress.

Accounts from survivors would also suggest that those who suffer the most are those who killed themselves as a form of escape from problems or situations that they did not have the courage to deal with, or as an act of spite towards someone they wanted to hurt. Too late they realize that they have brought their problems with them and that they have hurt themselves most of all.

Another interesting observation, especially from a family tree perspective, is that some suicide victims out of desperation attach themselves to some sensitive person who is usually a family member. This person then becomes burdened, depressed and finds themselves behaving in ways that are out of character. The story of Bernie that follows is included to illustrate how this might happen.

How can we help the victim?

Acknowledge the hurt and anger over what has happened but move on to a place where you can forgive the victim from your heart. Visualize then surrounded by the light of Christ and begin to send them loving thoughts and prayers.

Apply the ancient dictum, 'Hate the sin but love the sinner.' Since we don't have complete access to another person's mind we can never judge the victim but only the action. To judge the person is to invite judgment upon ourselves because as we judge so we are judged.

Be aware that you, and all those closely associated with the one who has died, will most likely be carrying the emotions that he or she couldn't deal with, like anger, guilt, regret, shame etc.

Give yourself permission to go through the experience of grief and feel the onslaught of emotions. It may seem as if you are going mad for a time but the only way out of the tunnel of grief is through. As we allow our emotions to come so will they go and whatever happens to be now is not forever. Where possible avoid the medication route. The pill that can cure grief has never been invented! Holding onto regrets, recriminations and unanswered questions keeps us stuck in the past and is a way of avoiding the grieving process that alone can lead to healing and resolution.

Understand that the greatest love you can show to your loved one is not by holding on but to let them go to the Lord. While this releasing may not be possible in the early stages of grief it should always be regarded as the goal. The spiritual bond between two people is not affected by physical death. However until the deceased is set free to enter the light neither party can be fully at peace.

A Suicidal Attachment

Bernie was a deeply troubled eighteen year-old who was being closely monitored because she was so suicidal. She had been to a counsellor who felt that the issues being addressed, while important, were being undermined by something much deeper. At fifteen she had left school but always felt that in so doing she had turned her back on her friends. From there on her life seemed to go from bad to worse, She bombarded herself with negative criticism, saying such things as, 'You're no good; you're useless; you're a disgrace to the family; why can't you be like so and so.'

What she had never been told was that she had an aunt who before she was born had committed suicide and that she had been named after her. This woman's story bore an uncanny resemblance to her own. At fifteen she had been forced to leave home and friends and go to England to look for work. There she was deeply unhappy and a few years later returned home. She became pregnant but lost the child. Her mother gave her a terrible time saying the same things to her that her niece was now saying to herself; 'You're useless; you're a disgrace to the family', etc. Bernie's mother had looked after her sister for several months before she died and now, caring for her daughter, it felt as if history was repeating itself. Another remarkable parallel between the two lives was that Bernie now had a boyfriend called Victor and her aunt, at the time of her death, also had a boyfriend with the same name.

Because of the stigma associated with the manner of her death Bernie's aunt was someone who was never spoken about and her niece knew nothing of her story. Yet, the nature of the secret appeared to be condemning her to repeating it.

Ancestral Scripts

Replicas

Ancestral scripts tend to pass in an unconscious manner from one generation to another. Because we are rarely conscious of them they replicate in our own lives and to a large extent we become the living embodiment of those who have gone before us. These scripts are what form our attitudes and are a mixture of positive and negative. Some of the negative ones are highlighted here in order that by becoming more aware of the influences that have shaped us we can now choose to shape our own destiny without the unnecessary baggage that could weigh us down.

Mary and the Baptist

One of the titles attributed to Mary the mother of the Lord is that she is the *Immaculate Conception*. In other words, she was conceived free from original sin. One way this could be understood is that from the beginning, and through the godliness of her parents Joachim and Anna, she was free from all ancestral and personal baggage. This meant that when the angel Gabriel appeared with the message to rejoice that she was 'highly favored' she could hear those words and respond with a total 'yes' to becoming the mother of the Redeemer. The path to her destiny lay open before her but also needed her co-operation to take it.

In contrast the words of John the Baptist, 'Prepare the way of the Lord, level the mountains, fill in the valleys, make a straight highway for our God' (Luke3:3-6) express our human reality of needing to bring healing to our past before we are free to move forward and embrace our destiny. The message of John who was the forerunner of Christ also provides a very powerful scriptural background for re-examining the many ancestral scripts that form so much of our core beliefs.

Once I was travelling from the south coast up to the border with Northern Ireland. It was five or six years since I had done the same journey and it had then taken me at least five or six hours to get there. This time with some vast road improvements it took just three hours. Travelling along I was very conscious of the enormous amount of work that had gone into carving a way through so many hills, filling up so many valleys and straightening up so many crooked parts in order to make a straight highway. I then began to reflect on how in our own lives we have inherited so many mountains, valleys and crooked paths that slow down our journey, impede our progress and affect our quality of life. To really hear that we too are 'highly favored' can be so terribly difficult when our hearts are weighed down by so many burdens that are not necessarily even our own.

Attitudes and Beliefs

We don't just inherit our ancestral genes, the crooked nose the bald-head or the bad temper. The real legacy of our ancestors is a whole set of attitudes and beliefs that have been handed on from generation to generation. Some of these are undoubtedly good but there are others that are well worth reflecting on because of how they impede our progress.

Take for example the belief that, *'People are not to be trusted'*. There are so many who go through their whole lives being suspicious and distrustful of others just because of that limiting belief that they have inherited. Someone may ask them for help and instead of digging deep they immediately think of ulterior motives. Is he or she genuine or do they just want the money for drink or drugs? Many never develop the noble virtue of generosity simply because they are so distrustful. Worse still, some even boast of their distrust as if it were a virtue instead of a cover up for meanness, which it often is. The bottom line is that the person who trusts others will always stand to gain far more than the person who is distrustful.

Another such belief that often has been passed down from generation to generation is, *'You are only as good as you are useful'*. In other words what we do, how well we perform, is the measure of our self-worth. The result is that many of us carry a sense of unworthiness and feel a sense of failure. We always think that whatever we do is not good enough and we should be doing more and trying harder. So we go through life beating ourselves up. Is it any wonder that so many die so quickly or have nervous breakdowns when they retire. If their work is taken away they feel that their lives have become worthless overnight. This also carries through into our relationship with God. We believe that he values us only on the basis of how well we perform and because our performance is never up to scratch we think that we live under his frown instead of enjoying his favour.

In many families there was the constant admonition to, *'Never rake up the past; leave it where it belongs'*. That one sounded good, if only it worked. Whatever gets swept under the carpet eventually wears through. The reality is that the past is never where we think that we have left it; rather we carry it with us until such time as we have faced it and accepted it as part of our lives.

In lots of families the script that was engrained in generation after generation was, *'What goes on here stays here'*. It was closely allied to, *'Don't wash your dirty linen in public'*. This promoted a culture of secrecy where people suffered intolerably in silence and no matter what was going on, to speak about it was to break a family taboo and was tantamount to betrayal. It was in such a culture that sexual abuse was able to hide behind a veil of secrecy for so long?

'Don't speak ill of the dead', was another unexamined script that many of us grew up hearing. Translated this meant 'never speak the truth.' Much easier to pray for the faithful departed rather than acknowledge the elements of their unfaithfulness. In Ireland we tend only to bury saints not real people. It is much easier to put someone on a pedestal and pretend they were something they were not rather than face how their behaviour might have left me deeply wounded. Failure to recognize my own woundedness means I will involuntarily pass it on to the next generation.

What I have mentioned are just a few of the hundreds of scripts that have been handed down to us in greater or lesser degrees. Because no one has ever stopped to examine them and expose them to the light of consciousness they automatically pass down to the next generation.

Scripts In Relation to Ourselves

'Who do you think you are?' – Don't believe in yourself.

'Don't forget where you've come from.' – Be limited by your background.

'Never let you left hand know what your right hand is doing.' – Be secretive.

'Be practical. Get your head out of the clouds.' – Don't have dreams.

'Don't be feeling sorry for yourself.' – Feelings are not allowed.

'I'll give you something to cry about.' – Tears are not acceptable.

'Wipe that smile off your face.' – Humour is outlawed.

'If you die with that face no one will wash you.' – Be yourself and no one will like you.

'Keep a stiff upper lip.' – Don't show emotion.

'You're too clever for your own good.' – Intelligence is suspect.

'Men don't cry.' – Don't be human, hide your tears.

'Control that temper!' – Anger is wrong.

'Why can't you be like….' – There's something wrong with me.

'Don't act above your station.' – Stifle your potential.

'Expect not and you won't be disappointed.' – Needs are wrong.

'Children should be seen and not heard.' – The voice of the inner child remains stifled into adult life.

'Who do you think you are speaking to?' – Always act inferiorly.

'Laughter always ends in tears.' – Pessimism is a virtue.

'We don't want extremes in this house.' – Avoid emotions.

'Cry and you'll cry alone.' – Tears make others uncomfortable.

'You're stupid.' – You always were and you always will be.

'You're no good.' – You'll have to prove yourself.

Scripts in relation to Family

'None of our family ever came to anything.'

'Our family has always been blighted with bad luck.'

'Don't dare bring disgrace on the family.'

'There are certain things we just don't talk about.'

Scripts in Relation to Money

'Money doesn't grow on trees.'

'Without money you are nothing.'

'Money is the key to freedom.'

'Money is the root of all evil.'

'When poverty comes in the door love goes out.'

'Always save for the rainy day.'

'The more you have the more you are.'

'Men control the money.'

'Don't spend; you never know what might happen.'

Scripts in Relation to Sex

'It's not something that we talk about.'

'It belongs in the dark.'

'It's embarrassing to talk about.'

'Parts of the body are shameful.'

'Sex is for procreation not recreation.'

'Sex is dirty.'

'Sexual sins are always serious.'

'Sexual thoughts and fantasies are wrong.'

'The woman is to blame; men can't help themselves.'

'Men are only after the one thing.'

'Menstruation is unclean.'

Nooses around our Necks!

'Some of us are given the awesome task of breaking our family's pattern of poverty, pain, suffering, ignorance, fear and so much more. Some of us come into life for the sheer purpose of guiding our family into a new way of thinking, living and being. For this reason, your family may think you are *weird* or different. They may accuse you of things that are not *right.* They may even tell you that what you are doing is *wrong.* You may feel that you *are wrong.* If everyone is content *going right* who are you to *go left*? If everyone in your family has made it through life in a cold-water flat *who are you* to want a town house? Should you find yourself in this predicament, stop trying to convince them *show them*!

We are living in a new age, a new time, when things must be different. You cannot continue to do what has always been done. *Something or someone must change.* It might as well be you! You have the vision. You have the opportunity. The only thing you need is the courage and strength to recognize that you have been chosen for this awesome task of implementing change. If you follow your own inner guidance, your progress will be the only evidence you need. Your life will provide a new direction for the generations that will follow you. Your job is to bring about change in a loving, gentle and harmonious way. You may have to leave some people behind. Should that be the case, bless them and keep on moving.

Until today, you may have been so loyal to your family patterns that you would not step beyond what you have been taught to believe. Just for today, dare to be different! Dare to introduce a new way of living and being. Dare to climb out of the family tree.'

The above piece is taken from Iyanla Vanzant's book *Until Today.*

Family Tree Quotes

'The past is never where we think that we have left it. Rather it is always
to be found wherever we are.'

Katherine Ann Porter.

'That which one generation chooses to forget another is forced to remember.'

Anon.

'Our lives reflect back to us those things about ourselves (and our ancestry)
that we have been unable to see, unwilling to acknowledge and unable to heal.'

Iyanla Vanzant

'The issues of the past that we refuse to deal with will always tend
to reappear as fate.'

Carl Jung

'History repeats itself, has to, nobody listens.'

Anon.

'Even though you have given up a past, it hasn't given you up:
it comes back uninvited and sometimes half welcome.'

Susan Glaspell.

'Not to learn from the lessons of history is to be condemned
to repeating them.'

Anon

'The truth that sets us free may also be the truth that first sickens us.'

Anon.

'How many are silenced because in order to get to their heart
they would have to scream.'

Ann Clark.

'Bring forth that which is within you or that which is within will destroy you.'

Gospel of Thomas.

'If you don't tell the truth about yourself, you cannot tell it about others.'

Virginia Wolf.

'Only that which lies hidden in darkness has the power to destroy.'

Virginia Wolf.

'Things come suited to their time.'

Enid Bagnold.

'Most new discoveries are seeing things that were always there.'

Susanne Langer.

'We find what we search for, or if we don't find it we become it.'

Jessamyn West.

'No man (woman) can know where he is going unless he knows
exactly where he has been and exactly how he arrived
at this present place.'

Maya Angelou.

'To be what we are, to become what we are capable of becoming,
is the only end of life.'

Robert Louis Stevenson.

'Only the darkness can judge; the light is always merciful.'

Anon.

'We seek the truth that is also seeking us, so we meet half way.'

Anon

'Blessed are those who know what they need to know,
when they need to know it.'

Anon.

'To tell the story of one is to tell the story of a thousand.'

Anon.

Discovering Patterns

A Practical Approach

Sight and Insight

The gannet is a magnificent sea bird with a wingspan of up to six feet. It is renowned for its diving ability and wonderful sight that allows the bird to see fish deep underwater from considerable heights. Here it is depicted in a reflective mode preening it's feathers. From reflection comes insight and this is captured in the image of the kingfisher.

Robert Louis Stevenson once wrote:

I keep six honest serving men, they taught me all I know.

*Their names are **What** and **Why** and **When***

*And **How** and **Where** and **Who?***

Drawing up a Family Tree is a quest for insight and involves a certain amount of reflection and research. This is usually the first step towards recognizing repeating patterns. All the essential questions are contained in the above quote. Where possible, the obvious people to ask are parents, grandparents and other members of the extended family. These are the ones from which the oral tradition of the family is most likely to be gleaned. Some stories associated with the family, may have become embellished with the passage of time but yet could contain some very significant nuggets of truth. For example 'My great grandfather died young and there was always a question over whether he took his own life or was murdered.' Clearly identifying the problems as expressed in the present generation, and having an eye as to what to look out for is also essential. In the above case it may well be that there is either a pattern of suicide or violence in subsequent generations that both points towards an answer and also indicates what needs to be done.

Identify any family traits, both positive and negative and see if you can relate them to your own life and personality, or to a relative you are concerned about. Is there anyone with whom you particularly identify or whose problems seem directly related to yours. As understanding is a vital ingredient of forgiveness, try to see the world through their eyes. Allow yourself to empathise with them in the choices they made and the actions they took. Ask yourself what might you have done if you had found yourself in their situation? A relative may have been deported to Australia on a charge of theft. The courage it took for that person to steal in order to feed their starving children may never have been acknowledged. A useful tip is to carry on a dialogue with a significant ancestor as if they were still alive, asking relevant questions, what they need of you etc. and also if you feel that they are bothering you, to respectfully command them to leave you alone. Ancestral influences often access our unconscious minds through our dreams, particularly at a time when we are seeking information. Be open to receiving relevant information in that way and make sure to keep a record of your dreams. In cases where information is difficult or impossible to obtain the 'dream road' can prove invaluable especially when used in consultation with someone skilled in that area.

Where an ancestor has been conveniently forgotten about and rarely given mention, it may be useful to visit their grave or go to a place that was special to them. In some cases the headstone may not even bear that person's name and it may be appropriate to have it inscribed. Lighting a candle in their memory and sending them loving thoughts is also a very valid form of remembering.

In many families a major cover up may be happening, and any attempt to 'dig up' the past will be resented. As a general rule the more an issue is kept secret the more potentially destructive it can be. On some occasions it may be necessary to look up public records but most vital information can usually be gleaned from older relatives and elderly neighbours who often have a great sense of oral history. Many people are inclined to run scared, probably through ignorance, especially if someone is very explicit about the purpose of their questioning. It may be no harm to remember that a lot of valuable 'trawling' can be done if approached in the context of a general chat.

Sometimes when family tree research is being conducted out of concern for a troubled individual, no pattern seems to emerge and there is no sense of identification between that individual and a deceased family member. Here it may not be the person's ancestor but some definite soul who is wandering in the 'borderlands', and trapped between two worlds that is causing the problem. They seem unable to ask for prayer or forgiveness and in psychiatric terms, as used by Carl Jung, they 'possess' the person and inflict their miseries on them. In Old Testament terms they 'visit' and in the language of the New Testament they 'trespass'. Where it proves difficult to identify such an entity some focused prayer on behalf of that person often has remarkable results. This approach is based on New Testament practice. When Christ named a demon He had control and could cast him out, but there were many instances where He did not name and yet exercised control. In His name we are empowered to do the same.

Drawing up a Family Tree – A Methodology

There are numerous different ways a family tree can be visually represented. From experience I have found that most of them are unhelpful and confusing. It is important that not just names and dates are represented but also to have a presentation that can allow recurring patterns to be identified. The following method is the one I have found that has served me well over many years and is my preferred one for use with clients. It was from work with Dr. Ken McAll the pioneer of Family Tree Ministry that I learned this simple method.

Beginning at the bottom of the page, place the names of the present generation in order of appearance, beginning with the eldest and down to the youngest. Include also miscarriages, abortions and early deaths, giving names to any who were previously nameless. Moving up to the next generation place the father and mother on the next line also in their rightful place as first, second or third born. Then continue the same procedure into earlier generations as far as possible using the information available. Next to each member of the family write down all you know about them and their life, include marriages, separations, affairs, careers, hang-ups, addictions their age and the way they died.

The following genogram provides valuable insights as to the various ancestral influences that are contributing to the problems experienced by Michael at the bottom.

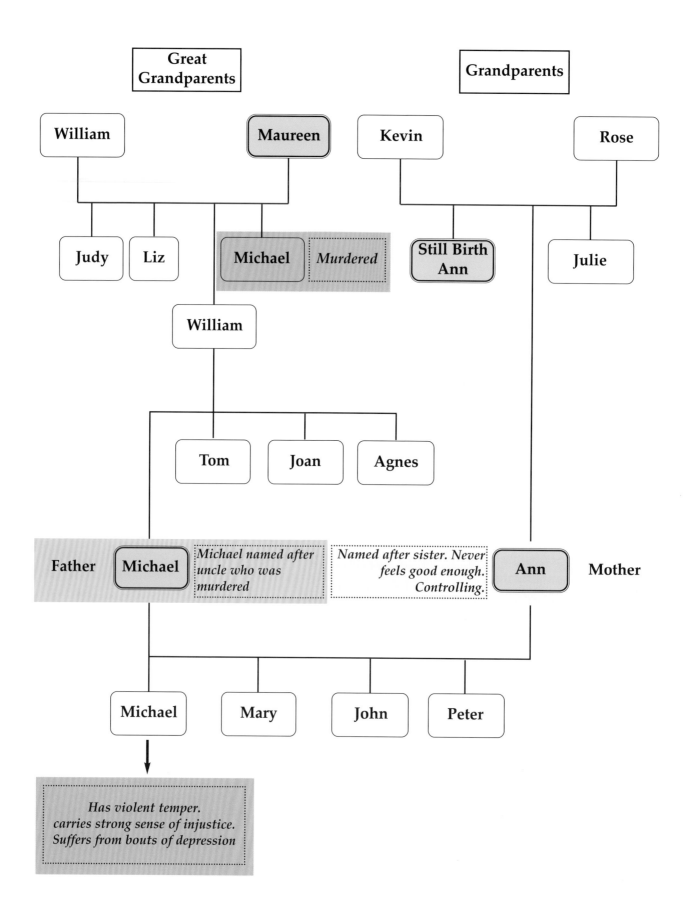

What to Look For in your Family Tree?

When drawing up a family tree for the purpose of healing it is important that it be far more comprehensive than simply having names, dates and placement.

Think of your Family Tree as a jigsaw and be aware of what parts don't yet seem to belong to the overall picture. Intergenerational Healing is about seeking out and finding the missing pieces and restoring them to their rightful place.

- Who in your family was least loved in life and least mourned in death?

- Who is least spoken about perhaps because they disgraced the family?

- Who died without being reconciled with family members or others?

- Who were the family most relieved to be rid of in death?

- Who died with bitterness resentment or other unfinished business?

- Who died an unhappy death and not at peace with themselves?

- Who was never given a Christian burial e.g body never found?

- Who is clung to in morbid grief by some family members?

- Who died young or tragically and his or her death was never got over?

- Who was locked away in an institution and disowned because of shame?

- Who keeps appearing in your dreams as if they are not at peace?

- Who died in exile, was drowned at sea, or killed in war?

Drawing up the Family Tree, look for recurring patterns passing down through the generations. Unredeemed history tends to repeat itself often in some disguised form.

- Problems associated with a particular name or names.

- A particular place in the family always associated with major difficulties e.g. the firstborn daughter, the second born son, the youngest etc.

- Someone in each generation who is the Blacksheep, possibly the most vulnerable one, who acts as the Scapegoat carrying the disowned shadow side of the other family members.

- A troubled individual born close to the death of a troubled ancestor.

- Onset of symptoms coinciding closely with death of ancestor.

- Recurring sicknesses, hereditary diseases, idiosyncratic behaviour.

- Patterns of addiction. eg. alcoholism, gambling, eating disorders.

- Early or sudden deaths, stillborns, miscarriages, abortions, suicides.

- Unhappy or childless marriages, forced or unacceptable marriages.

- Violence, criminal behaviour, unacceptable behaviour.

- Physical, emotional, spiritual or sexual abuse.

- Injustice in earlier generation causing sense of victimisation in others.

- Poor resolution of conflict. Rows over wills, land, property etc.

- Occult involvement, morbid interest in the diabolic.

- Unresolved grief in one generation influencing subsequent generations.

- Illegitimacy and parents not taking responsibility for their offspring.

- Pattern of children being 'farmed out' to other relatives.

- Poverty in one generation giving rise to materialism later.

- Accidents and recurring patterns of bad luck.

- Psychological disorders e.g. schizophrenia, paranoia, anorexia nervosa.

- Sexual identity problems, sexual deviancies, abuse etc.

- Family groups and homes associated with coldness in their relationships.

- Restlessness, always on the move, or being forced to move.

- Serious problems arising in family after acquisition of property or land.

- Patriarchal or Matriarchal control, where one persons influence continues in an unhealthy manner, even after their death. In many families such a figure stands as a colossus and their memory is deified as if they could do no wrong. A deeper examination often reveals that such an individual may have been cruel, tyrannical and very controlling. Placing them on a pedestal is a defence mechanism that shields the next generation from looking at how they have been wounded by this person. In not recognizing their hurts they in turn unconsciously inflict their problems unto another generation.

Early Questions

Growing up on a remote farm in County Wexford, there were many questions that occupied my mind from a very early age. Looking back it was probably these that formed the basis for my interest in this area of healing the past. For most of my young life I wondered why we always seemed plagued with what seemed to be bad luck. This took the form of crops failing and animals dying continually, usually for no apparent reason. During those years we experienced hardship of every sort, and a general inability to make progress no matter how much effort was made. When at the age of eleven, my father died suddenly, my mother, who had no previous farming experience took over and immediately remarkable changes began to take place. In those six years, and with a lot less effort, the farm prospered and remarkably, not one animal died. Clearly this stood in marked contrast to what had been happening in previous years where on average animals were dying at a rate of often one per month. With the takeover, it was obvious that a major shift of another nature had taken place but to what could this be attributed?

On the day after my Father's burial I clearly remember my Mother praying out loud in desperation in front of a picture of the Sacred Heart. There was no money, having grown up in a town she had no experience of farming, and suddenly she was a widow. Her prayer was one of absolute surrender, a handing over of all that had gone before and a profound act of trust in God and Providence for what was to come.

The exact nature of what had gone before and its implications for what had been happening became clearer to me as I grew older. When I was two years old, a series of sudden deaths had wiped out my father's entire family in just six months. It was a cruel blow from which he never recovered. Those who knew him well said that he became a shadow of his former self. Up to the time of his own death nine years later, it would appear that he was still holding on to those he had loved and lost. Living in the past also meant that his farm was 'stuck' in the past, and his inner association with death found outward expression in the crop failures and animal deaths.

All it took was the simple prayer of a heartbroken woman to break the pattern. Only when the past was left behind could a more prosperous future unfold.

Personal Story

Connections – Letting in the light – Creativity

The photo above shows three turned pieces of wood. The first is a series of spheres within a sphere to which I have given the title *Looking for Connections*. The second is a Latticed Pomander, which I associate with *Letting in the Light*. The last one is a twelve-pointed star inside a sphere, this I call *Releasing Creativity*. Each one reflects different stages of the journey towards healing of our Family Tree. My own story told from the maternal side illustrates this process.

One of the findings of genetic science is that males take on more of the genetic characteristics of their mothers while females take on their fathers. In my own life, I identified far more with my maternal line and my investigation into that side of the family has yielded some very interesting connections. Starting first with my grandfather, much of his adult life was spent with the Irish Lights Service stationed on a lightship called the Conningbeg, The light from this vessel I have seen almost every night for twenty-five years from my bedroom window since it is positioned directly off Kilmore Quay where I have been 'stationed'.

In his early life my grandfather was a seaman and from my childhood days, listening to his stories, a great love of the sea and quest for adventure was born in me. However there was also another side to his time at sea which he never spoke about. On one occasion a man was killed in an accident caused by the negligence of some members of the crew.

Five of his comrades conspired against my grandfather to have the blame pinned on him. As a result he had to leave that ship in shame and the unresolved anger over that event characterised him for the remainder of his life.

In the years after his death I found that I was burdened with a sense of shame, the root of which I could not find in myself. It was as if that shame, although felt by me, did not belong to me. It was this awareness which made me realise that there was unfinished business from my grandfather's time which was spilling over into my own life. I may have inherited his love for the sea but I also had inherited something else! This resulted in me standing proxy on his behalf and forgiving the five men that were responsible for framing him. Having done this, the burden of shame lifted immediately. Once the connection was made and the root cause identified it was a relatively simple matter to resolve the issue.

The person with whom I have an even greater affinity and a deep sense of gratitude towards is my great grandfather also on the maternal line. This may seem remarkable since he had died a long time before I was even born. Most of my life as a priest has been spent in Kilmore Quay. It was there that he was born and reared before moving to Wexford where he was employed as boat builder in the local dockyard. Here he was highly regarded as being a genius with wood. As foreman he was involved in the building of a boat called the *Guillemot* which was one of the first reasonable sized boats to fish out of Kilmore Quay. This survived until 1998 and was the first boat I ever took a trip on as a teenager. Tools were not easily available in those days, many craftsmen had to make their own. The tools of his trade were passed on to his Son, my grandfather, who, having no male heir, passed them on to me. Prior to my appointment to Kilmore Quay I was involved in the building of a boat using many of those same tools. In four generations the wheel had come full circle.

Reopening The Wells

In the Bible it is mentioned several times that a custom of the Patriarchs was to re-open the wells dug by their forefathers. Such a practice is deeply symbolic of what happens in the process of ancestral healing.

It was in relation to my great grandfather that I discovered one of the great positive aspects of praying for one's Family Tree. By putting to rest unfinished business we are opening the well and in so doing are releasing the positive heritage of our ancestors. Their gifts and talents are also ours to benefit from. Up to my mid forties I had lived with awareness that my creative side was severely blocked. However, just after doing some ancestral work I began to feel more and more drawn towards working with wood. After converting an old garage and buying a lathe I started turning wood with results so amazing I was even surprised myself. Never having seen anyone turn wood before, and with absolutely no tuition, I found that I could produce quality items from the beginning and with very few mishaps. It was as if I had been working with wood all my life. Clearly it was a gift from my great grand Father, which had been waiting to be released and was now mine to enjoy. More and more I have found the use of wood in giving retreats and seminars to be a powerful 'visual aid' in the work of healing and the in the presentation of the Gospel.

Cup and saucer with mustache facility
Once owned by my great grandfather

Symptoms of Ancestral Bondage

What signs would we look for that might suggest a problem with our ancestry and not just something arising from our own life that is calling for attention? The following is a list of possible indicators:

- Recognizing a pattern recurring through several generations.

- More than one member in a family affected by similar problem.

- Sense of not belonging in the family.

- Onset of symptoms close to death of ancestor.

- Troubled person born close to death of ancestor.

- Family secret or secrets being closely guarded.

- Something or someone never spoken about truthfully.

- Poverty consciousness. No prosperity. Resources always strained.

- Sense of bad luck. 'If we kept ducks they would drown'!

- Medical problems that don't respond to conventional treatment.

- Identification with ancestor. One life mirroring another.

- Every blessing becoming a curse.

- Symptoms having a visitation nature. Not always constant.

- Troubled ancestor appearing in dreams.

- Resistance to talking about the family history.

- Dreams with an ancient or ancestral quality.

- Behaviour that is uncharacteristic of the person.

- Irrational thoughts and actions.

- Inability to move forward in life.

- Restlessness, wandering, discontentment.

- Compulsive behaviour pattern.

- Pattern of accidents that keep recurring.

- Simple things going terribly wrong.

- Recurring injustices. Always being the victim.

- Present event mirroring and awakening old issues

- Overall sense of sadness and despondency.

- Having a family scapegoat who gets blamed for everything.

- Feeling trapped and burdened.

Jung and the Unconscious

The Swiss Psychiatrist Carl Jung (1857-1961) was distinguished for his investigation of the unconscious and it was he who coined the terms 'personal' and 'collective' unconscious. From his teaching it is clear that he believed that there is a clear interconnectedness between human lives that continues beyond the grave. It's not just what happens to a person in this life but rather how he or she responds to the events of life that will affect future generations. It would appear that in our personal unconscious we have the capacity to sum up within ourselves the emotional make up of our ancestors down through the ages. In the collective unconscious, the experiences of all past generations of the human race are buried. Where a conflict is not resolved in one generation it is then passed on to future generations. Unresolved issues often seek a physical outlet and so find their way into our tissues. Many hereditary diseases may be the body's way of expressing what has not been said in an earlier generation but is still crying out to be said. The symptom itself therefore, if understood as the particular form that the problem chooses to manifest itself, may provide the most valuable clue as to what is seeking expression.

Ancestral Identification

In his work, *'The Archetypes and the Collective Unconscious'*, Jung wrote of, *'States of possession in which the possession is caused by something that could perhaps most fitly be described as an ancestral soul, by which I mean the soul of some definite forebearer. For all practical purposes such cases may be regarded as striking incidences of identification with deceased persons. Naturally the phenomenon of identity only occur after the ancestor's death.'*

He goes on to say, *'In the structure of the personality, there are ancestral elements which under certain conditions may suddenly come to the fore. The individual is then precipitately thrust into an ancestral role. In primitive psychology ancestral roles play a very important part. Not only are the ancestral spirits supposed to be reincarnated in children, but also, an attempt is made to implant them into the child by naming him/her after an ancestor.*

Many primitives also try to change themselves back into their ancestors by means of certain rites. Ideas of this sort date back to the Stone Age and it is not improbable that these primordial forms of experience may recur even today as cases of identification with ancestral souls, and I believe I have seen such cases.'

A case of 'identification', where one life mirrored another was that of Philip who was named after his grandfather. At 18 he fell deeply in love with a girl who broke off the relationship after six months. He developed a jealous obsession with her which later led him to suffer a nervous breakdown. He later stole money from his employer and ended up being sent to jail. While inside he spent some time in solitary confinement and there became very aware of the presence of his grandfather who had died long before he was even born.

This Philip from an earlier generation had in fact died in jail. As a child he had lost his mother and as a husband he was extremely jealous and became violent towards his wife. One night while under the influence of alcohol he murdered her and was later convicted and given a life sentence. He too had spent time in solitary. The awareness of what he had done drove him insane because fear of losing what he treasured most had caused him to kill the one he loved. After only three years in prison his heart literally broke and he died of a heart attack.

The parallels between the two lives were quite obvious and the later Philip found himself almost literally walking in his grandfather's shoes. A simple exercise of cutting the harmful ties between the two of them proved very useful in helping him overcome his obsession and move on to meeting someone else and rebuilding his life.

Family Tree – Stories Of Healing

The following are a series of stories drawn from many years of ministry. They are chosen and commented on because each one shines a different light of understanding on the subject.

Inherited Bitterness

'My Grandfather had a row with neighbour over land. He died with great resentment and this was a legacy he passed down to my father who also died a very bitter man. Now I feel that same bitterness in my bones and am very aware that if I don't do something about it, it will pass on to another generation'.

Bitterness that is bred in the marrow will come out in the bone!

A Burdened Substitute

Jenny's Story: 'I am 44 years of age and have been diagnosed with two tumours, one of which is inoperable. I feel quite well, and find it difficult to believe that I have only a few months left to live. Could there be any connection between my condition and the fact that I was named after my mother's favourite sister who died tragically before I was born. Her family and my mother in particular never let her go, and tended to treat me as a substitute for her. I feel as if I have been carrying someone else on my back all my life and that the burden has become too much'.

It would appear that ancestral issues can get into our tissues and eventually form part of our genetic makeup.

Conflict Brewing

'There has been terrible conflict and trouble in my family for many generations. Recently my mother died and the whole family is up in arms again. I seem to be bearing the brunt of it and feel very rejected. I have had several Family Tree Masses offered but nothing has changed. How do I see myself in all of this? Very much the victim, the scapegoat. I'm now becoming embroiled in a legal battle, which I can ill afford. I'm wallowing in self pity, I'm full of negativity and I'm avoiding the rest of my family like the plague.'

The above account is not a success story. In this case having Family Tree Masses offered seemed to make very little difference. It is a good example of how not to go about family tree healing. It is obvious that very little personal work has been done and the person involved, while looking for answers, seems not prepared to make the changes necessary within herself in order that she might become a channel of healing and forgiveness.

Ringing for Attention

Margaret's mother lost her only son at 33 and never got over his death. She developed a ringing in her ears and a fuzzy, dizzy head, which caused her to sometimes lose her sense of balance. Since her mother's death Margaret has developed the same condition and more recently her daughter has begun complaining of the same symptoms. All three of Margaret's family suffer from severe lower back trouble with two of them having operations on the same day.

Symptoms can be very accurate signposts.

A Future Awakens

'Fifteen years ago I did some research and had a Mass said for my Family Tree. Over the next few years my life underwent a complete transformation. It seemed as if many of the obstacles that were blocking my path of destiny had been removed. I have since studied psychotherapy and currently have my own practice.'

Healing usually takes place gradually and almost imperceptibly.

Inherited Trouble

'My father was very involved in the Troubles of the 20's. I suspect he died with a lot of blood on his hands. Ever since his death I have been very burdened and in poor health. I have also noticed that all the families around here who were likewise involved have somebody 'not right' in every generation'

This is a classic case of how the sins of the fathers get passed down.

Dis-eases of Grief

'I have suffered bad health for over twenty years and have been continuously in and out of hospital. I have Lupus, acute renal failure, a kidney transplant, which later failed and now dialysis. My mother and I are strangely linked; she had two miscarriages before me and three after me. She also lost two brothers at 7 and 8 and later her sister at 19 just a month before she was due to get married. After that her father died and three years later her mother. I feel that I have been carrying so much grief for her that my sickness is the result.'

Here an intolerable legacy of grief is finding physical expression.

The French Connection

'All the members of my family have always had money problems. My house is now on the market for seven years and there is no sign of a buyer. For a long time I found myself repeating the few French phrases that I know and wondering why did I not become fluent in French rather than Italian. Also, whenever I saw a long necked, bejeweled, elegant lady I often heard myself saying 'send her to the guillotine'. My family research reveals that my mother's side came from France, just after the Revolution, where they were involved in the guillotine operation. After arriving in Cork they set up a money lending business and were noted for their cruelty in extracting money from their clients. My strange 'French connection' and even my money problems are only now making sense.'

Much of what is mysterious about the present has its roots in the past.

A Mother Substitute

'My father took his own life when I was 9 years old. Our relationship was almost too close. I was the emotional substitute for my mother who was involved in another relationship. For at least three years after his death I heard him screaming at me as if for help. Through counselling I tried to let go of him but still felt him around me with the sense that his death was only yesterday. Using visualization I realized that he was the one holding onto me. I commanded him to go towards the light but his shame and remorse held him back. His mother came out of the light and tried to coax him but to no avail. Suddenly my other grandmother appeared whom he got on well with. She was always forceful by nature and her approach seemed to work. He turned from me and together they walked into the light. For the first time since I was a child I can sense freedom in my spirit.'

Not everyone we let go of lets go of us. They may have to be told.

Payback Time

'From a very early age I was 'farmed out' to an aunt and uncle where my grandmother who was bedridden for 30 years lived. She became my responsibility and for years I looked after her every need. Every night I tucked her up in bed put Johnson's baby powder on her four pillows and 4711 on her hankie. In counselling I have been reclaiming my childhood lost through minding Granny and I have also been looking at the issues, which left her crippled with arthritis for so long. I responded to a Gerry Ryan invitation to tell stories about smells which remind you of childhood. The prize was a holiday for two in the French Riviera. I have never had a holiday in my life and after leaving down the phone I said 'Gran this is payback time'. Shortly later the phone rang to say that I had won the holiday.'

By making inner connections we create outer surprises.

Providence to the Rescue

A girl was getting married and intending to take over the family pub business. As far as anyone in the area could recall no first-born male child in that public house had ever survived. Needless to say this was a matter of grave concern especially if she were to have a boy of her own. Where this pattern originated no one could tell until providence intervened in a most remarkable manner. At the conclusion of a seminar in Co. Cork two women came forward and in a discussion about Wexford mentioned this pub. I immediately asked what they had heard from their father who obviously knew the place very well. Legend had it, he had told them, that during Cromwellian times while a mother was breast-feeding her first-born baby, a soldier fired a shot through the window and killed the boy.

When sincerely seeking the truth it comes to meet us half way.

The Missing Parts

Margaret had always had a strange affinity with her great-grandmother after whom she had been named. This woman had been evicted with eight children. Her husband's relations took over the farm and the resulting bitterness resulted in the breakup of the marriage. Seven of those children emigrated to the U.S.A. Margaret had lost six parts of her body in various operations and was threatened with losing yet another part. It was as if she were mirroring in her body the losses suffered by her grandmother who as she had watched her children leave had lost so many parts of herself.

Some connections make sense but challenge our beliefs.

Closeness Beyond

For several years a woman was troubled by very bad dreams and nightmares. These always featured her father and went back to his death. He had been a violent alcoholic and had a terrible relationship with his family. Slowly she began to understand the cause of his problem and came to forgive him. After a Mass was said for him she began to feel a great sense of peace. Her dreams then changed dramatically and she began to see him as a very warm protective figure. In fact from there on she claimed to have a much better relationship in death than she ever had in life.

Good news! It's never too late to form a good relationship.

Emotional Desertion

'My grandfather was murdered during the time of the Land League. He left a widow with six children. She was unable to cope and deserting her children ran away with one of the workers. One of those children was my grandmother who, never having been mothered herself, had a terrible relationship with my Mother. She in turn had a poor relationship with both my sister and me. My own relationship with my daughter began to turn cold and distant; so with the help of some praying friends I brought the entire family history before the Lord in prayer and within a very short time the relationship improved dramatically and has been close ever since.'

Emotional coldness runs in families but it starts somewhere.

Legacy of a Dark Secret

Rory was a man of 36 who had never known a day's peace in his entire life. He had come from a good home with loving parents and wanted for nothing but even as a young child he remembered being deeply troubled. 'I feel as if I'm carrying something that doesn't belong to me; it's like I or somebody belonging to me has killed someone,' he kept saying. He was named after both his grandfather and his great-grandfather. Family research revealed that the latter had been very involved in the political struggle for Irish freedom. As well as being an informer he had committed at least two murders but someone else had taken the blame. The man had gone to his grave carrying this dark secret. Clearly Rory was carrying the burden of guilt and injustice, but why him and not any of his siblings? At one level he was carrying the name and very likely he was conceived as a twin with the other lost early in the pregnancy. As tends to happen with the surviving twin there is often a legacy of guilt where one feels responsible for the death of the other. This then mirrored the ancestral issue and acted as a hook upon which it could rest.

All other therapeutic interventions had been tried with no success in this case. It was from a place of utter despair that Rory began to look at the wider picture and find answers.

A Painful Reminder

Margaret was a woman in her 60's who had serious hip problems that an operation and other medical treatments had failed to help. She had been named after an aunt who at twenty-four was knocked off her bicycle by a reckless driver. The handlebar had gone into her body just above the hip. She suffered ill health for a few years and then died. There was a lot of resentment and a sense of injustice surrounding her death. As a young woman her niece Margaret one day went behind her house in the dark and severely injured herself just below the waist by walking into a plough handle. Later she also fell off her bicycle and suffered a broken leg. Now once again it was her hip that was causing problems and refused to heal. The deeper wound had to be addressed first. Forgiveness was needed and her aunt was prayed for and then very quickly the hip responded to treatment and came right.

Sometimes the deeper wounds cry out to be healed first.

Cover up and Suicide

Six suicides over a period of twelve years was more than any family should have to bear. Two of these were young people who died before they were even teenagers. Most family members sensed that something was seriously amiss while those who had children feared for their future. Tracing the history of the tragedies, the first was reasonably understandable. A daughter who was very close to her father had died at a young age. She didn't cope with his loss and always said that she wanted to be with him and so took an overdose. The mother got married again, to a man of a violent disposition, and set up house taking her youngest son with her. The other children were more mature and stayed in the family home. The young son was known to be the object of his stepfather's jealousy and one day his elder sister found him hanging, but in a manner that seemed quite suspicious. The police didn't pursue the matter largely on the basis that there had already been a suicide in the family. Drawing together all the evidence, some of which took years to emerge, the balance of probability strongly suggested that the child had been murdered in a fit of rage and it had been made appear like a suicide. The destructive power of the secret seemed to act as a gaping hole through which four more relatives were to fall before the truth was finally spoken.

Many flounder on the submerged rocks of family secrets.

Inherited Sadness

Fiona thought for many years that she had a major problem coping with her husband's anger. Eventually she persuaded him to come with her for counselling. On the way a serious row developed and the fallout continued into the session. From the dynamics at work between them it was very evident that Fiona had a far more serious problem with her own anger than with her husband's. Slowly, after a period of shouting and screaming, she was able to admit that her unhappiness ran far deeper than her marriage. At one stage she expressed a view that 'she had been born sad' which paved the way for deeper questioning.

Her mother had been previously married to a man whom she had deeply loved but who had died within a year of the marriage. The time of Fiona's birth coincided with the anniversary of his death and this was when the mother always went into serious depression. "He left me. He abandoned me" were the expressions she had always heard her mother use in relation to him. Being quite sensitive Fiona had absorbed this sadness and throughout her life had continually found herself thinking about this man she had never known. A deep awareness formed that a link had been established between her and him through her mother. She also saw how much of her mother's unlived life she had been living out. After cutting the ties between herself, her mother and this individual, a number of remarkable changes came about:

Her shouting, screaming and even screeching at her husband and children stopped immediately.

She felt different, relaxed and more peaceful, yet beginning to question her own identity apart from the burden she had carried for so long.

Every time her husband was leaving home, even to go to work, she had felt that he was leaving or abandoning her. Such an irrational reaction had always puzzled her, but now made perfect sense in the light of carrying so much emotional baggage from her mother's loss.

Relatives used to describe her as suffering from the 'doormat syndrome'. Vulnerable from the beginning she had suffered physical and emotional abuse as a child from other siblings and as an adult she was still in the victim mode. Now for the first Fiona began to assert herself.

We can either fix the blame or fix the problem! We can't do both. Once Fiona stopped blaming her husband, he was now free to constructively deal with his own issues. Prior to this, his anger always awakened hers and they inevitably became embroiled in conflict with both parties blaming each other. Three years later, each having learned to take responsibility for their own reactions, they now enjoy a very harmonious relationship.

Grief Awakening

Peter was a wealthy property developer. When at the height of his career his wife got a serious illness. She recovered, but shortly afterwards he had a nervous breakdown. His mother had died six years earlier and his father the same year. At the time Peter had been drinking heavily and he drowned his sorrows in whiskey. Since his breakdown, ten years had passed with no improvement. He has been in and out of psychiatric care on numerous occasions and the last resort being offered was electric shock treatment, something that he was very reluctant to take.

Peter's mother had been married for eight months and was six months pregnant when her husband was tragically killed. She eventually remarried and the child grew up extremely close to his mother but viewed with jealousy by his stepfather. At an early age her son apparently took his life but there was always a strong suspicion that he was murdered. One of the men with him on the night was later charged with another murder. His mother never recovered and Peter grew up very aware of his mother's pain and of being a substitute for her son and husband.

The sickness of his wife was the trigger that awakened the trauma over his mother's death and all that she had carried to her grave. Over the years, what had been trying to break through into consciousness was being blocked by strong medication, and Peter knew that it was making him worse rather than better. For a long time Peter had a recurring nightmare of being thrown out of his bed onto the floor. Viewed symbolically his right to his own private space was continually being denied him. To have his own identity was impossible because of what he was carrying from his mother.

In this case one grief awakened not just another but so much of what was unresolved in relation to the other.

Marital Unrest

Hilda and John were married for thirty-five years. There was always some unease in Hilda regarding their relationship. At one level she had no doubt that she loved him and he was a genuine and fine person. Yet at another, something was compelling her to break free and make a life for herself. This came to a head when they both reached retirement age and John's preferred option was to remain in the city while Hilda was adamant that she wanted to live in the country. The matter brought them to the brink of separation. Hilda then remembered that her Grandmother, whom she was named after had lived a very unhappy life in an arranged marriage. Economic circumstances meant that while she always wanted to break free she never could. This realization of how she was identifying with her grandmother made Hilda understand her irrational behaviour and became the key to resolving their differences. It was a classic case of one person unconsciously repeating the fate of another.

The Family Gifts

Ian Cullen

As a child I believed everything that was told to me. When I grew up I discovered a completely different family history from the one that had been planted in my mind. Our parents had eight children and each one has a completely different recollection of our shared and fragmented past. This is mine.

In our family history there is an abundance of good fortune and tragedy. The tragedies include, cancer, brain hemorrhages, sexual abuse, divisions between parent and child, sibling rivalry, addiction, loss of wealth, mental illness and losing children to adoption. The good fortunes came from a sense of idealism and justice, prominent positions in politics, creative thinking, strong personalities, resourcefulness, family identity, tree planting, astute business acumen, winning the sweepstake and then winning the first Irish 'Ideal Home' in the 1950's. Our family was blessed by all this.

Then our home (the 'Ideal Home') became the subject of an Irish precedent of law. It was the first time an Irish son and an Irish wife had taken a father to court over their rights to reside in the family home. The man was my grandfather and it was determined that he was 'unreasonable of mind'. I inherited both his name and his gift. But, I also inherited gifts from my other grandfather and from both grandmothers. The main issues directly affecting my life have been loss, separation, mental illness and addiction. These are recurring themes in at least three of my grandparents' families. They have continued to repeat throughout the generations.

The German word 'gift' means 'poison'. If we can examine our poisons we may accept them and discover the treasures that they bring. In our family we have been reluctant to acknowledge and accept these gifts.

Then four years ago I began to attend Family Tree Healing nights in Kilmore Quay, not knowing what to expect. During these last four years the energy of our family has changed in a steady, positive and wholesome way. There has been healing in our relationships to each other and a greater sense of well-being throughout the family. Proving such results is almost impossible but the changes do coincide with the family tree healing work. In the beginning I wanted to drag my whole family down to the sessions and get everyone fixed. Then I realized that it was enough for me to ask, observe and witness events within the family and let the other members proceed in their way. I made certain choices, sought direction and advice and researched the family tree, with all its secrets. I met as many relatives as I could. People appeared out of the woodwork as if by chance to help with information and anecdotes. It was like an airing of an old linen before folding carefully and storing it away again. But I did learn that we cannot drag other people into the process against their will. The intention is to heal rather than hurt and I was reminded of this many times along the family tree journey.

FAMILY TREE – STORIES OF HEALING

My brother's wife was so overwhelmed by the amount of recurring illness and bizarre patterns of behaviour in our family that she jokingly called it the family soup. Now we have started to acknowledge our crazy family soup and we are finding great nourishment within it.

Great rewards can be enjoyed when we start the process of healing our family tree and great comfort too, when we start to accept and embrace our family gifts.

A Family Divided

Brendan Mullins.

The Divided Homestead

The following story of a long-standing family disagreement began on a farm just a few miles from where I grew up. The remains of the dwelling place as it stands today are shown with its decaying form mirroring the ancient division. It is a good example of how the unfinished business of one generation gets passed onto another. The son Brendan Mullins who has been committed to bringing about reconciliation for over sixty years gives the account.

As the story goes:

My father married in 1918. It was part of the marriage agreement that a dowry of £150 would be paid to his father who would then sign over the farm to his newly married son. This arrangement worked well for some years until my aunt, his sister, Mary, dissatisfied that her brother had been given the farm, went to her solicitor to try and have the agreement broken. It was discovered that the words, 'goods and chattels' had been omitted from the legal document. She thereby claimed that all the stock and farm machinery belonged to her. The times were poor, she felt hard done by, and I have no doubt that sheer poverty was her motivation. After all there were just the two of them and she felt entitled to something. A few nights later, along with her two brothers John and Pat, she came and removed horses, cows, cattle, pigs, hens and all the machinery to her farm. The row had begun. Shortly afterwards my father, infuriated by what had happened, along with a friend and two neighbours went and brought everything back home. The two brothers John and Pat wanted no more feuding and returned to Liverpool the next day, The following night Mary and her husband confiscated everything yet again. The travel weary animals were back on the road the very next day when my father and a group of neighbours did a raid and returned them once more. At this point another neighbour spoke some words of advice to Mary about the matter and everything stopped.

Back home in the midst of all the turmoil my mother was trying to cope with three small children, the youngest, Anastasia, being just six weeks old. With the cows missing there was no milk but local women helped out by bringing food and milk. Anna took seriously ill with a stomach upset and died within days. It was believed that the change of milk was the cause, helped no doubt by all the strife that was going on around her. At the time the custom was to give the baby only the milk from the best cow and that a change of milk could have serious repercussions.

My father blamed his sister for the child's death and bore a deep resentment towards Mary and to a lesser extent towards John and Pat. Unwilling to forgive, the hurt and anger bound him, and he took much of it out on his eldest son Nick. The stand-off continued for thirty years so I grew up not knowing my uncles or cousins even though we lived just miles apart. Then in the mid-fifties my father, while at an auction, pointed out his brother John. Sensing a softening of heart I went over and introduced myself and then proceeded to bring John over to my father. They both clasped hands and with tear-filled eyes lamented the wasted years. The next day John brought his brother Pat to our family home and the past was talked about and all three were reconciled.

My aunt Mary was still out in the cold but after months of struggling with the issue my father eventually agreed that I should contact her. This was done on Monday and a meeting was set up for the following Sunday. It never happened; she died unexpectedly two days later. In fact she was being offered the hand of reconciliation even as she was dying even though she was unaware of the fact. At her funeral on the Friday my father said in sadness, 'Now it will never be healed.' I tried to reassure him that when we make up our minds to forgive, then forgiveness has already taken place.

As the story continues:

My father came to his death with unfinished business. The burden of regrets from the past made it difficult for him to let go. For too long he had allowed anger and hurt to define who he was. How he had treated his son Nick also weighed heavily on his mind. Nick had been the target of my father's displaced anger and so became the family scapegoat who got blamed for everything. He went to England and broke contact with the family, returning only once for our mother's funeral. There he lived a wayward life and died an early death still estranged from his family and very hurt by his father.

During a time of prayer, Nick, by now ten years dead, came strongly to mind with the conviction that I needed to pray for him and seek out his grave in London. I sensed that it would be an outward journey symbolizing an inner need to re-establish the connection between us.

Having said 'yes' to going, Providence immediately came into play with an amazing set of coincidences. Next day I was handed a free car ferry ticket for two. On leaving the dock we noticed that the road we were on was the same as the registration number of our car which seemed to confirm that we were on the right track. We had a rough idea of where Nick had ended his days but no idea as to where he was buried. The receptionist at the hotel where we booked in gave us the number of the local priest who agreed to say Mass for Nick the following morning. Not only that, but he knew exactly where to direct us in order to find the grave. A short time later I was standing at my brother's lonely, unmarked grave and all my unresolved grief began to overwhelm me. At that moment I was the other brother ready in my heart to welcome the prodigal back home and delighted that together we could walk into the banqueting hall.

As the story panned out:

After the initial estrangement, the two sides of the family went in separate directions. Children were born to both parties in the disagreement and most of them never knew the family story. They lived and died only vaguely aware that they had first cousins and not even knowing their names. The core of the hurt was over a little girl who died from a stomach complaint, whether the change of milk had anything to do with her death no one knows. What we do know is that serious stomach conditions have afflicted at least four females of the later generations.

After putting his story in writing Brendan expressed the following wish: 'After eighty years of estrangement it would be wonderful for those of us who have lived with the fall out from this hurt all our lives to meet and agree to finally put an end to such a contentious issue where neither party was right or wrong but both sides were very seriously hurt. If this were to happen, I feel that we would be opening a door for the souls that may be still out in the dark to come in, and, I even think that the angels in Heaven would rejoice with us that peace has finally been restored.'

As the Story Concluded:

The Mullins' story became the subject of an R.T.E. series called *Flesh and Blood* and was shown in early April 2006. This took the form of telling the story in the context of an open letter read by Brendan Mullins to his long lost relatives inviting them to meet and put an end to the age-old division. Later in the month a young man was killed tragically in a fall from a horse and he was a relative of the other side of the family. After the funeral a woman called Mary came and embraced Brendan. She introduced herself as the daughter of Brendan's estranged aunt Mary. Her brother then came and one by one introduced Brendan and his wife to their long lost relatives, most of whom were at the funeral.

It was the decisive moment of reconciliation that had taken over eighty years to come about. Very significantly where it finally took place was in a graveyard, the place where the earlier reconciliation of Mary and her brother had originally been intended over thirty years earlier but had never happened because of her death. Peace had finally been restored.

A Compulsion Exposed

Ray was a hard working, well-respected, and well-liked member of his work team. After struggling for years with a compulsion to expose himself it eventually began to happen in his place of work. This seemed completely out of character and came as a major shock to everyone including his boss, who immediately referred him for therapy.

There was nothing about his life's story that would indicate why this should be happening. As to when it began he clearly remembered that it was just after the death of his grandfather, whom he was named after. This man was well known to have fathered a handicapped child that he disowned. While this was common knowledge he himself lived and died in total denial, oblivious to the deep hurt he had caused to both the child and her mother. Now it seemed that the sexual sin that he had tried to cover up all his life had taken on the form of compulsive sexual exposure in his closest grandson.

The resolution of this problem was reached by this young man coming an understanding of why he was suffering in this manner. It was also a crucial step in the healing process that he sought out that rejected girl, who already knew the facts, and on behalf of his grandfather apologized for the way she had been so shabbily treated.

Incest

Sarah was a woman of South African origin who had spent many of her earlier years working as an 'escort'. Now she had changed careers and was a successful businesswoman dealing with high finance. Although she believed, based on her own experience, that the sins committed in the board-room were far worse than those committed in the bedroom, she still needed to come to terms with and integrate her past.

She was aware that her life closely resembled that of her grandmother's. She too was a lady of the night before marrying a wealthy politician. They had two children but the political life didn't suit her wilder nature and so she separated from her husband. The pattern of sexual dysfunction continued into the life of her two siblings with the brother having sex with his sister and a child being born of that union. Sarah's mother bore the blame and was made an outcast by the family. She then left South Africa and came to live in England where Sarah grew up. At a young age her mum walked out on the family leaving Sarah to carry the maternal mantle.

In attempting to investigate her family background, and allowing that story to be told, Sarah travelled to South Africa. There she met relatives who helped her piece together many of the missing pieces of the family jigsaw. One important detail she uncovered helped to shed light on her grand-mother's behaviour.

Apparently her grandmother had been the victim of incest by her father who was the governor of a jail in Durban that was notorious for its cruelty. In her life she too had been a victim and was acting out in a sexual manner that which had been inflicted on her. An important part of the healing process was for Sarah to stand proxy for her grandmother and forgive the hurt caused by her father.

In seeking understanding as to where she had come from, Sarah was able to understand much more clearly who she was and why she had behaved in the manner that she did.

Speak Not – See Not!

Rita was 74 she began to experience problems with her lower jaw. It became increasingly difficult to open and eventually almost locked making it very difficult for her to eat or to speak. Her daughter, several years earlier, had experienced a similar problem and this had rectified itself immediately when a Family Tree Mass had been offered for one line of her ancestors where there had been incest followed by the murder of a child. Interestingly, her distant relatives had requested this Mass and she was freed from her affliction without any awareness of what had taken place. Another sus-pected part of the family pattern was Rita's elder sister who for some years had suffered from drooping eyelids. One was having difficulty talking and the other had problems seeing.

Rita revealed that on his deathbed at seventy her father, a very troubled man, had called for a neighbour and requested that his family be never be told about what had happened. The 'what' became a matter of curiosity and conjecture for many years. The evidence available seemed to point to her father having fathered a child by a young Protestant girl who worked in the house. A court-case was threatened and a settlement was made out of court. However the man went to his grave having made a very deliberate decision to turn a blind eye and refuse to speak ever again about what had happened. Perhaps, given the level of anger he carried, it is possible that he never managed to forgive himself.

Now, many years later as his daughters reached a similar age, it was one daughter who still couldn't open her eyes to look and the other who couldn't open her mouth to speak. In this case a significant recovery began as soon as the connection with the past was recognized and a resolution made to have a Mass offered for those involved.

A Legacy of Injustice

The final piece of this section, Our Ancestral Inheritance, belongs to a story given to me shortly before I sat down to write.

Fifty years ago Margaret became pregnant by her second cousin. Her family were staunchly Catholic, highly respected and considered to be pillars of society. She was deemed to have brought disgrace on the good name of her family and was duly banished to England where her child was born. Unable to support the baby and herself she was forced to place her daughter in an orphanage. At fourteen she reclaimed the girl and they lived together for the next thirty years. Margaret then returned to Ireland where she died six years later. Nuala, her daughter came home for her mother's funeral where she was treated as if she never existed. She was given no recognition by her relatives as their niece, cousin, or as her mother's daughter but only introduced as a friend of Margaret's.

Somewhere in England Nuala continues to live out a lonely existence. She never married and her isolation is made so much worse by the fact that she does have relatives who out of misguided loyalty to their parents choose to treat her with the contempt she dies not deserve.

Margaret and Nuala's story typifies yet again the consequences of splitting off aspects of reality, whether they are people, events or emotions. It shows all too clearly how so many similar situations were dealt with in the past and why the legacy of injustice that remains to the present day stands urgently in need of healing.

Homecoming

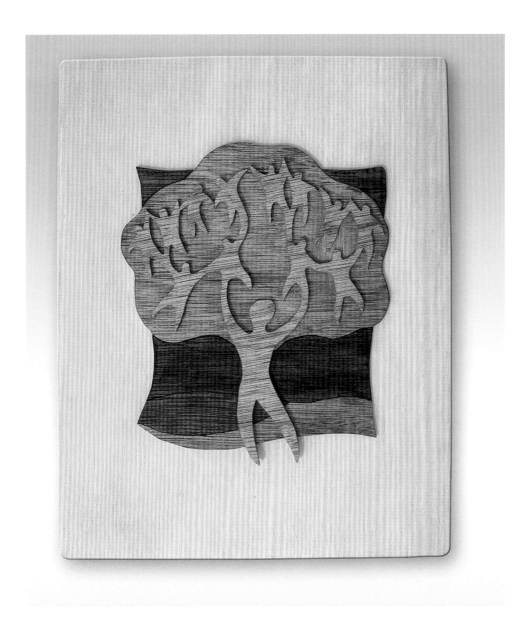

Giving everybody their proper recognition and restoring them to their rightful place in their family of origin and in God's family is what Family Tree Ministry is all about.

PART 2
HAUNTINGS &
HAPPENINGS

Hauntings

Strange Imaginings or Strange Happenings?

Bill was invited by friends to a party at their country house. When he arrived he found a large number of guests at the villa. A lot more than lemonade was consumed and towards the end of the evening the host came to Bill and said, 'My dear friend I have no option but to put you up in the haunted room since all the rest are full'. 'That would be my pleasure', said Bill who wanted to impress the ladies who were looking on admiringly and saying, 'Aren't you bothered about the ghost? Don't you know that a poor woman who committed suicide thirty years ago still walks there?'

Soon Bill was lying in his pyjamas on the bed in the haunted room. Just in case anything might happen he had left on a small light and had his revolver on the bedside table. As he was dropping off to sleep he suddenly noticed five small dark fingers slowly moving at the end of the bed. Bill opened wide his eyes, closed them and opened them again.

The five small dark fingers were still there......and all at once there were ten of them. Bill raised himself slightly. 'Stop your silly game,' he said. 'Show your face or I shoot.'

Coolly and calmly he seized his revolver. The little hands moved almost beseechingly, but no face came into view. 'I shall not say it again', he called. 'On the count of three I shoot.' The ten little fingers began to tremble. 'One' called Bill. Two. Three.' He pulled the trigger. Since then Bill has been lame in one foot!

While many ghost stories are no doubt the product of fear and a fertile imagination there is a compelling body of evidence that would suggest that paranormal activity is a reality in many people's experience and in some cases it can even be scientifically verified.

Lights that go on and off on their own. Footsteps on the stairs. Scraping sounds in the attic. Tapping in the walls. Trinkets and keys that vanish. Fresh food that suddenly spoils. Cold spots that raise the hair on the back of your neck. Things that go bump in the night.

These are some of the most common signs of a house affected by a restless spirit or negative psychic energies. Even among the most hardened sceptics there are a surprising number who reluctantly acknowledge such chilling paranormal events. One estate agent who doesn't believe in ghosts tells of entering a vacant house where he felt something violently tugging at his sleeve. Other houses he claims have a 'vibe' so bad and so strong that he refuses to cross the threshold.

People go to enormous lengths to eliminate every logical explanation for these feelings and occurrences. They call the plumber or the electrician; they blame it on stress; they put it down to an over-active imagination. To concede that supernatural happenings are taking place is always the last resort. Many manifestations were happening in a guesthouse I was once familiar with. Yet help was not sought until three sets of visitors all from different countries reported seeing ghostly figures clad in clothing of a by-gone age. All three descriptions matched perfectly.

Many are aware of a spirit presence in their home and treat the matter with a certain degree of curiosity. They speak of the spirit as being quite harmless and are quite content to settle for co-habitation. It's the living we need to fear and not the dead, is the belief often quoted. However, in such houses there often seems to be an abnormal amount of sickness with family members being prone to accidents. Many happenings are attributed to bad luck and constant financial pressure often characterizes such families. In one instance prayer and the celebration of the Eucharist failed to dislodge a restless spirit. In this case it was the soul of a seaman who returned after many years to find his home taken over by others. He died in poverty and bitterness with the issue of the eviction still unresolved. Why he refused to move on when requested only became apparent when the lady of the house admitted that she was happy to leave him there. A year later she was diagnosed with cancer. The property was then sold and she moved to another location.

While visiting a hospital in Toronto a Native American patient told me of an interesting custom that was practiced in his tribe. If a member was deemed to have died with unfinished business and not at peace it was widely believed that he could continue to affect the place where he had previously lived. To counteract this a miniature replica of the person's dwelling was made and placed on his grave in the belief that in the spirit world size was no longer of importance and the spirit would still feel at home.

In a recent study conducted by two business professors at Wright State University, what they class as 'stigmatized ' or 'psychologically impacted' houses take 50% longer to sell and go for a lower rate than average. In cases where gruesome, high profile murders have taken place the selling price understandably drops by 15-35%.

It is interesting that California State law now requires that any murder or violent death that's occurred in a residence in the past three years must be fully disclosed to a potential buyer. Also the Supreme Court of New York has upheld the premise that a house can be haunted and that it can affect the future expectations of sale.

Paranormal investigators find their services increasingly in demand. Many use such basic tools as a non-contact digital thermometer to detect cold pockets, an electro magnetic field detector, a compass, as well as audio and video recorders and a 35mm still camera. Once a presence has been detected it is followed by research into the property's history in order to establish the spirit identity and the cause of its lingering presence. A boy of fourteen once showed me a very clear picture, taken on his camera phone, of a very distressed woman, who had been brutalized in his home. This woman, it was believed, had never forgiven her husband and was not at peace.

A common misconception is that only old houses are subject to psychic disturbance. In many cases the site, or the surrounding area, that the house is built on provides the key to understanding why manifestations are happening. It may be that the original site was an old farm from which occupants were evicted or where the ownership had been in dispute. Likewise a site that was associated with tragedy can appear to be responsible for psychic contamination continuing to be a feature of the new building.

The Parallel Dimension

A tragic mistake, based mostly on ignorance, often made in the past was to banish troublesome spirits to the depths of the sea, to faraway places or even to hell where they could no longer cause problems for the living. This often took the form of an exorcism performed on the site. The presumption was that such spirits were always evil. Little consideration seemed to be given as to why the spirit or spirits were seeking help and why they were still so attached to a home or to its contents. In many cases individuals may not have come to terms with their death and were trapped in a parallel dimension. Instead of banishing such spirits the Christian approach should always be to commend such spirits to the Lord in prayer and encourage them to journey towards the light and join their loved ones on the other side.

Sick Building Syndrome

Not just individual homes but public buildings often used for civil administration are often characterized by psychic contamination. 'Sick Building Syndrome' is a term that is becoming more and more recognized. This is characterized by a high rate of absenteeism; high rates of depression and addictions; workers irritable and often in dispute; bad decisions being made; headaches and tiredness; non-productivity and inability to meet deadlines. In some of these cases tests conducted revealed high levels of radon gas, thus providing a natural explanation for the symptoms, but in the majority of cases the cause had to be looked for elsewhere. In one public building, that was once a notorious jail, half of the building had been added at a much later date. Here the absenteeism rate in the older building was double that of the new and this was the case year after year.

Symptoms of Contamination

What are the implications of living or working in a house or building that is psychically toxic? These are some of the more common symptoms:

• Tiredness and lack of energy that is not experienced elsewhere.

• A sense of oppression and lack of creativity.

• Loss of clarity. Not being able to think straight.

• A sense of claustaphobia that eases when one goes elsewhere.

• Debilitation and recurring health problems.

• Moodiness, irritability and despondency.

• Children often exhibit hyperactivity and have problems sleeping.

• Avoidance of parts of the house that are most affected.

• Sense of being watched, sometimes by shadow like forms.

• Not feeling safe. Having to leave the light on at night.

• Irrational behaviour patterns.

• Feeling decidedly uncomfortable.

• Being easily startled for no apparent reason.

• Disturbed dreams and nightmares.

• Cold areas that never seem to warm up.

• Sense of being caught in a time warp and not able to move forward.

• Lack of prosperity and strained resources.

• Coldness and lack of affection between family members.

• Accidents, breakdowns and malfunctioning of equipment.

• Illness, disease and deaths.

A family that is unfortunate to purchase such a house may find that the past history of the place begins to replicate itself in their family story. A previously united couple may begin to experience marital problems and end up separating. Children may become attention seeking and teenagers might well engage in anti-social behaviour. A previously successful business conducted from home may go bankrupt. Sickness, tragedy and hardship in the past may well result in tragedy and heart-break in the present. At an even more serious level where a place was associated with death and sadness the history of the new family may well begin to evolve along similar lines.

Sensitive Souls

A particular area of difficulty, not well documented and even less understood, is the long-term effect on babies or sensitive young children who sleep in areas that are psychically contaminated. In some cases adult depression, for which there is no apparent explanation, may well have its origin in having begun to absorb negative energies from such a young age and continuing to do so later on in life. This is often noticeable in a well-adjusted family where members share a secure background and a similar history. The depressed individual is often found to be the one who slept in the bedroom that nobody felt comfortable with.

Closely related to the above is the story of Muriel who up to the age of eight was a lively, vivacious, care free, fun loving child. Then overnight she underwent a personality change into the antithesis of all she had been; moody, depressed, fearful and tearful. Her doctor could find no medical reason and she referred her to a child psychiatrist who was equally baffled. One question unlocked the mystery; had she by any chance changed bedrooms? The parents nodded and their eyes lit up with recognition that this had indeed been the case and her problems had coincided with this change. For twenty years the father's mother who had been crippled with arthritis spent most of her time in that room. The child had never been close to the granny and wasn't grieving her loss. However the newfound symptoms were very similar to those that characterized her grandmother over the years of her confinement. The recognition of what was taking place, a simple prayer with the girl and a blessing of the room was all that was required for a complete and immediate return to normality. In that room there had been no signs of abnormal activity nor was there any reason to suggest that the woman was not at rest. Perhaps the energy generated through so many years of suffering was a legacy that remained and had its impact on the girl. In cases such as this the ancient practice of blessing a house or room after someone dies is borne out as being very wise and well worth holding onto.

Practical Guidelines

Where para-normal activity is suspected or evidenced there are a number of lines of enquiry they may prove useful to follow. It is important not to jump to the most obvious conclusions too quickly. An accurate identification of the problem is necessary before a solution can be reached.

First it may be important to try and make the sometimes difficult distinction between whether the problem is being caused by a ghost or an earthbound spirit. A ghost is not really a person but rather a psychic imprint left in that place by someone who once lived there, perhaps suffered a lot, and may have died traumatically. Their spirit or essence may already have passed on to a higher dimension. Such residual negative energy can usually be dispelled with a simple blessing. Also it tends to fade with time especially when newcomers bring their own positive energy. An earthbound spirit, on the other hand is a real person who has not moved on after death as they should have done and needs help in order to do so.

If the house is built on limestone there is a possibility of Radon Gas causing problems. A simple test can check this out.

Were there any similar problems associated with the family prior to moving to this house? If there were, this would indicate that the issue has more to do with the family and their history than with this particular place.

If the house is relatively new was it built on an earlier site? If so, what is the history of that earlier dwelling?

Is the house situated in an area where other dwellings are experiencing similar problems? If so the problem has a wider dimension.

Is it built on an old burial site or where an ancient battle took place?

Does the land carry a history of eviction or disputes over ownership?

If several generations of the same family lived in the place take a close look at their history and how it may be replicating itself in the present generation.

What was the history of the previous occupants? Was there discord or violence that gave rise to a disturbed energy? Was there any occult involvement like séances or tampering with ouija boards? Was there ever a suicide or murder committed, or was there ever an eviction from the place?

What can be Done?

Inclusion

At first sight the piece illustrated represents a Resurrection Cross. It is also the picture of an invisible figure forming an opening at the heart of the Cross.

In Christian belief the Cross of Jesus is the place where forgiveness is found and the doorway to eternal life is opened. Bringing the troubled soul to the Cross in prayer is the key to releasing them to continue on their journey. In the context of the Eucharist, which makes present to the unseen world the reality of Calvary, that soul can be cleansed from sin and find the doorway into eternal life.

It is in this context that the practice of having a Mass offered for the deceased finds its true meaning. Being present to intentionally pray for and commend the person to the Lord would follow as an integral part of encouraging that soul to move on and join the saints in the light.

Restless Spirit

The events described in the following story were witnessed by all four family members. What was their cause and how could they be explained?

Lights dimming in the living room with the chandelier shaking. A change of electrical fittings made no difference.

A shower being turned on and off without anyone being near. An electrician was called in but could find nothing wrong.

A television losing the picture for several minutes and then coming back.

A heavy large double bed being shifted a considerable distance in the room.

A cold presence moving through the hallway.

All the manifestations seemed to coincide with the death, and particularly the burial, of someone in the area. In between times everything was normal. The strange happenings were noted to have begun with the death of someone who had lived for a short time in the place. This man had been badly brutalized as a child by his father. In an act of revenge he returned as an adult and tried to burn his father to death while he slept by setting fire to his bed. The attempt was unsuccessful and he fled back to England. There he went to live with a prostitute and found one day that his bank account had been emptied. He returned home and in the course of a vicious row she knocked him out with a blow from a hammer. Some time later he recovered and in his rage murdered her and then took his own life. Neither of the two bodies was ever claimed.

Viewed symbolically what was happening with the lights could be understood as the spirit of this man being unable to face the light. The shower might point to a need for inner cleansing from guilt while the efforts to restore the television could point to the need for someone to get the picture. The moving bed issue had the obvious connection with the attempt on the old man's life but since the bed represents the place where we rest it also suggested that it was his soul that was not at rest. Something that also added extra validity to this was the fact that it was when local people died and were being laid to rest that these manifestations were at their worst.

All the indications pointed to this one individual, troubled in life and not at peace in death. His partner and father were also part of the picture and could not be left out when his soul was being prayed for and commended to the Lord.

Present Realities
Mirroring Past Events

Mirror Image

The above piece is a natural edged yew bowl showing two star shaped cracks almost identical on each side and mirroring one another. It provides a useful visual image of how the past can be mirrored in the present both at a personal and at a collective level.

How the past may continue to influence the present in ways other than the obvious is, to say the least, mysterious and to many quite scary. Yet there is a Biblical tradition of reconsecrating places that have been desecrated through blasphemy, violence and the shedding of blood. The Christian Church has a very strong tradition of using holy water and blessed salt in prayer for protection and in the blessing of places and land, particularly those that have been associated with tragedy and what we usually regard as 'bad luck'. It is also an integral part of the Catholic tradition to have Masses said for the dead and to pray for the souls in Purgatory. The implicit implication in these practices is that past and present are so interwoven that the healing of one is the healing of both.

Problem Parishes

Dotted around Ireland especially in rural areas are numerous examples of what could be classed as 'problem' parishes. In many cases, priest after priest, or other community leaders who have worked or ministered there have suffered depression and mental breakdown and often gone to an early grave. All too seldom is the parish viewed in its historical context where it often becomes quite evident that a burden of history has broken the spirit of whoever may have been in charge. Many such places are characterised by a lack of openness, emotional coldness, resistance to change and a seething resentment that can burst forth at any time and sabotage any initiatives that are being attempted. Also it is not uncommon to find that the suicide rate in such parishes is way above the national average, early deaths are all too frequent and a large percentage of families being dogged by hardship, sickness and bad luck. Sometimes a pocket of unredeemed or unhealed history is still the driving force in such places and while it's long gone underground it is still engaged in what amounts to guerilla warfare. In areas that were subjected to bloodshed and strife the ancient dramas may well have continued in a different manner down the generations on different stages and with different actors. With a bit of insight we can often see quite clearly how the past mat be alive and well in the present. The simple acknowledgement of such past events and bringing them before the Lord in the Eucharist for healing, along with prayer for those involved, is a wonderful way to remove the past from the present.

The Bermuda Triangle

If, as Carl Jung believed, the personal issues of our lives which we refuse to face and deal with, come back to haunt us as Fate then the same principle must hold true at wider collective levels. Certainly one of the most fateful areas of the world for centuries has been the infamous Bermuda Triangle. Many volumes have been written on the various bizarre happenings that took place there over centuries when ships and planes would disappear, often without trace, in mysterious circumstances, and with alarming regularity. Back in the Seventies the English psychiatrist Dr. Ken McAll spent some time becalmed in the area and intrigued by the mystery began doing some historical research on its history.

From the logs of sea captains who plied the seas in the days of the slave trade, McAll was able to discover that over two million slaves had been thrown overboard in that stretch of water. These unfortunates were part of the largest forced migration in human history, an enormous crime against humanity that was considered legal for three-hundred years. Estimates of numbers vary from ten to thirty million. They had been snatched from their homes and loved ones, often having been betrayed by their own kin, and forced to endure a nightmarish voyage across the Atlantic Ocean. The conditions that these slaves had to endure almost defy the imagination.

These unfortunates were chained together and packed like sardines on shelves no more than eighteen inches deep and often deprived of food and water for days. Reports of the time state that whenever the ships doctor would go below to tend to someone he would frequently pass out with the stench of human excrement and the suffocating lack of oxygen that was so great that even candles could not be lit

Drawing close to their destination, in the area of the Triangle, it was customary for the human cargo to be reviewed. Many of the Africans would have perished on the voyage, often with their corpses still chained to the living. Others were found to be in a very weak condition and not worth keeping, and so these too were thrown overboard and only the strongest kept for the market. McAll also discovered evidence of a marine insurance racket whereby compensation was paid for loss of cargo enroute. Thirty pounds per slave was the going rate for a long time, a considerable sum in those days. Naturally it suited the profiteers to 'lose' as many as possible, not just to obtain compensation but also in the process to keep up the current market price for their commodity.

In response to those findings, and in consultation with the a local Anglican Bishop a number of Eucharists were offered where the souls of the forgotten were committed to the Lord and an apology was made for those responsible for the murders and atrocities. Hearing of this event at the time, many adopted a rather skeptical 'wait and see' attitude. Now over thirty years has elapsed and we have neither seen nor heard of any more strange happenings. The carefully maintained coast guard records of inexplicable events in the area effectively show a blank from that time and so the area has disappeared from the news.

For Those With Eyes to See

The repercussions of the Chernobyl nuclear disaster continue to shock the world. Is it not significant that the site of one of the world's greatest disasters was originally a concentration camp and burial ground? This was an area already psychically contaminated by unimaginable human suffering and destined to erupt and pollute the Ukraine bringing untold hardship and suffering to so many.

If viewed in the context of the age-old enmity between England and France, Princess Diana's untimely death can be seen in a much different light. Could it not be significant that the 'Rose of England', the 'Princess of Hearts', as she wanted to be known, should lose her life while travelling in a French vehicle through an underground tunnel in Paris, the heart of France? Perhaps at a deep level a collective desire for revenge wanted to strike a blow at the heart of England and if so it certainly succeeded.

Was it purely coincidental that in Ireland in 1945-47, the Famine centenary years, the T.B. epidemic was at its height, when once again the country groaned in travail and almost entire families were wiped out? One grim reality seemed to be mirroring another even worse.

Over twenty-six years of the Northern Ireland conflict, a pattern was quite discernible where so many of the areas associated with conflict and battles from earlier times, became once again, the scenes of other, terrible atrocities. The different layers of history were very similar in nature.

The Time Warp Effect

On a more local level, dotted around the country are innumerable homes, farms and small areas, which carry their own pockets of painful, or even shameful, history. They now appear as if locked in a time warp, where in spite of the best will in the world, together with unstinting effort, hardship is unrelenting, progress never seems to be made, and prosperity remains but a dream. Similarly it only takes a small amount of research on many of our own family trees to see patterns repeating through many generations. It would appear that not only do we inherit the genetic material of our forbearers, but we can also be blessed with their characteristics and burdened with some of their problems and unfinished business.

In so many respects we are products of our own individual past, of our family of origin, and of the country into which we are born. Our 'Shadow' side therefore has many facets, which include personal, familial and political elements. Could it be that the past exercises more of a hold over the present than we care to imagine? If it does, then recognizing what has gone before is of vital importance, and praying for the 'Souls in Purgatory' takes on a whole new meaning, importance and urgency!

The Land is Sullen!

The above expression was used by an old man in relation to the land he had worked on all his life and to the neighbouring lands that stretched around him for two or three miles. 'One year there's a bumper crop; the next it yields about half; after that it's likely to fail completely. The good result you get one year, you end up paying for it the next. It's the same all around these parts. There's got to be something wrong somewhere?' Running through that area is a fine straight road but notorious for accidents along a stretch of several miles. Many local residents also seemed to be blighted with tragedy and bad luck. Young people in particular seemed to be the ones most affected.

Many inhabitants of the area reported having witnessed strange happenings, psychic disturbances and ghostly appearances. In some fields animals avoided certain spots and horses took fright if driven into those places. Animal deaths were unnaturally common. Several householders even believed their homes to be haunted.

Running through the area was a military road and to facilitate its construction all the people in the once well-populated area were evicted from their homes for a considerable distance on either side in order to ensure that soldiers would have freedom to march without threat of attack. No consideration was given for the suffering caused, homes were burned, lands were confiscated, and people were made homeless. At least two serious battles were fought in this region with certain place names still bearing evidence of this. More than once the people were subjected to murder, rape and pillage by soldiers who went on the rampage after winning a battle.

All the present realities pointed to past events for their explanation. A Eucharist was offered in the area where the past was brought before the Lord, prayers were said and apologies offered for what had taken place. Some individuals stood proxy for those who had been evicted and offered forgiveness towards those responsible. Because the entire area had been so desecrated part of the service was a reconsecration of the area to the Lord.

Resulting from this were some almost immediate changes. Within weeks the local council decided to light up the area of road where most accidents had taken place. A man who had grown up there who knew nothing of what had taken place reported noticing a remarkable change in the atmosphere of the area when he returned home and how his father seemed more contented than he had ever been. Also, two brothers, who were landowners and natives of the place, came together and made peace after being alienated for most of their lives.

The situation will still need to be monitored over a period of years to see if the pattern of accidents and tragedies has been broken and if people are beginning to enjoy an acceptable degree of health and prosperity.

Our Maritime History

An Episode Redeemed

S.S. Ardmore

On June 12th 1998 a final chapter was written not in relation to a family but to a ship called the S.S. Ardmore, which had been lost some miles south of the Saltee Islands in November 1940. The painting of the vessel is by the well known marine artist Brian Cleere. With twenty-four men aboard and a cargo of cattle she had sailed from Cork and was on passage to Fishguard in Wales when she struck a mine. There were no survivors. For many years her whereabouts remained a mystery and she was thought to have sunk close to Wales. In recent years divers from Kilmore Quay, with the help of local fishermen, were able to locate and positively identify the wreck. A memorial Eucharist was held in Kilmore Quay with over one hundred relatives of the crew taking part. These came from the four corners of Great Britain and Ireland. As each name was read out a relative, on behalf of their loved one, rang a bell with a gong recovered from the Ardmore wreck and last used on board the ship. Each later received the Bread of Life from a dinner plate, which acted as a paten, and was last used at the crew's table on their last voyage.

On the day prior to the service a local man made a remarkable and highly providential find. In an old scrapbook, which had been compiled by his late mother, was a newspaper report of a bottle having been washed ashore on Curracloe beach just north of Wexford, a few days after the tragedy. This contained a message written in pencil on the back of a Goldflake cigarette box saying 'We are sinking fast, please send help'. A number of the crew had signed their names with 'S.S. Ardmore' written on the bottom. For some reason news of this find had never been communicated to the next of kin and hearing it read from the altar was like a message from beyond the grave, only this time help was at hand.

After the service the relatives took a boat trip to the site of the wreck, which was marked by a large buoy that was secured to the boiler of the ship. The main purpose of this was for each to lay a wreath on behalf of every man who perished. One crewman's son sprinkled clay from his mother's grave saying that she had carried this mystery to her grave. Another man who had lost two brothers said that he had been at sea all his life but that this was his most difficult and yet the most important voyage of his life. Perhaps the most significant and freeing moment of all came when many of the relatives began to acknowledge a deep resentment held since that time towards the captain. He was known to be in a hurry to get back to Liverpool in time for his daughter's wedding and had set sail on a stormy night when other ships were seeking shelter. It was not known that the vessel had hit a mine; it was believed that she had floundered in heavy seas and for this they held the captain fully responsible. It was unanimously agreed that in order to close the chapter on such a tragic episode the final words had to be forgiveness towards the Master.

A Garden of Remembrance

Remembering the Past
Living the Present
Shaping the future

Following the commemoration event for the S.S. Ardmore and seeing the healing impact on relatives after so many years arose the concept of developing a Memorial Trail and Garden dedicated to people who had lost their lives at sea. This was opened in 2001 in Kilmore Quay and has since become one of the major attractions in the South East not just for tourism but also more as a sacred space for reflection. Using nautical symbols combined with the natural landscape of the area it now reflects the universal journey of loss. In what was once the village dump now stands a sunken ship built of stone. After walking the trail the visitor is invited to take hold of a huge ship's wheel as a symbol of resuming responsibility for his or her life after loss. The plinth beneath the wheel is inscribed with the words, *Homeward Bound*. In front there is a fountain, a compass and a large bronze propeller blade that resembles a ship's sail. Symbolically these speak of getting back in touch with life, especially inner life, checking direction and setting one's sails in order to move forward. Before the mast are hundreds of names of those who were lost at sea. As we complete our grief journey we carry them and our loved ones forward on our voyage through life. In remembering the past and living the present we can now shape our future.

Each year in June a commemorative service is held for all those lost around our coast. People from all over Ireland attend. Each year new names are cut in stone. Many have loved ones who were lost and their bodies never found and so the Garden of Remembrance replaces the grave they were denied. In this simple manner an opportunity is provided for, *Remembering the Past and Empowering the Present.*

An Oceanic Experience

M.V. Oceana

In April 2003 an event took place that I have to rank as one of the most memorable spiritual experiences of my life. With hindsight I believe that it was a direct and natural extension of remembering and praying for those lost around the coast of Ireland.

While doing chaplaincy service with the Apostolate of the Sea, Mission to Seafarers on board the P&O vessel Oceana, I was crossing the Atlantic and positioned almost exactly mid-ocean just south of the Azores. A Eucharist was being celebrated in the mess room for the crew who were mostly of Indian origin. These were men and women of extraordinary and vibrant faith the like of which I have rarely encountered. It was this quality of faith which I have no doubt was to create the conditions favourable for what was to take place. No mention was made, nor was thought given, to praying for those who had perished at sea. At the Consecration everyone became aware of a profound movement of the Spirit. Many began to shed tears, some went into silence, yet others saw visions which, when shared later turned out to be remarkably similar. In essence this visual imagery amounted to a giant vortex opening in the ocean and reaching down to the depths. Out of this there appeared to be thousands of souls streaming upwards towards the light. The consensus was that these were souls who had perished in these waters, no doubt over many centuries, and who had not yet found their way home. For nearly twenty minutes the celebration ceased while those who could see with their inner eye watched until the crowd ended with some stragglers looking bewildered and surprised to have finally made it. They quite literally had nearly missed the boat! There were many of the crew who saw nothing, but all were quite aware that something profound was happening and so they responded with deep prayer. These were men who when their contract was expired would move to other ships and sail other seas. Their experience that night would have left an indelible impression and an awareness that wherever they sail they have a ministry, to remember in prayer and bring to the Lord those who have lost their lives at sea.

Such a faith experience lies far beyond words and is difficult to put into words. There is always the risk of it being misunderstood. Here it is shared in the context of a ministry that had begun in 1998 with a memorial service for the relatives and crew of the S.S. Ardmore lost so many years earlier. I like to think that their voyage of disaster in 1940 resulted eventually in a voyage of discovery for so many in 2003.

Commemorative Goblet

The wood for the above goblet was found at a hot spring near Ponta-del-Garda in the Azores the day after the event described above. It was turned as a way of representing the vision and commemorating all those whose souls had risen from the depths of the ocean the previous night.

PART 3
POLITICS &
RELIGION

Remembering

The Truth shall set us Free

Tabernacle of Truth

Remembering is a sacred action. It is the way of integration and of becoming whole. It stands at the core of the Eucharistic Celebration, 'Do this in memory of me.' As such it is the key to bringing about change and transformation. At a personal level the things we try to blot out of our memories always diminish us while at the wider level the issues we have tried to forget find a way to come back and haunt us.

In recent years, as a society, we have been struggling to come to terms with the horrors of institutional abuse. For far too long the unimaginable suffering that was inflicted on the most vulnerable was not spoken about while those who were most affected were denied a voice. They had little option but to suffer in silence and in so many cases were forced to bring their secrets to the grave. Yet their silence cries out to be broken and unless the door is opened and the past revisited there can be no healing. Only in the story being told and the truth heard can integration take place. So long as the pain of the past remains unacknowledged it will cry out for vindication with the potential to overshadow future generations.

Unfortunately the untold stories will always far outweigh the ones that will be told. The annals of history don't give much space to the underdogs and the nobodies. Yet there are more and more individuals who are reclaiming their voices and finding the courage to speak. In the story of each one who can be heard we are also hearing the story of countless thousands whose truth never could and never will be heard. It is they who are the voice of the voiceless and the ones who are most deserving of our ears and admiration.

Our Political Past

Cross in Tree

The cross shown has not been tampered with in any manner and was found deep inside an old tree that grew in the heart of one of the Wexford battlefields of 1798. It was only after the tree had been felled and split into blocks for firewood using a mechanical splitter that the remarkable discovery was made. It is even more remarkable that it survived the cutting and splitting process and emerged so perfectly framed. Upon close examination a silhouette of a slender figure can be seen on the cross while the texture resembles dried blood.

Our Political Family Tree

Historians remind us that almost no episode of Irish history has had such enormous influence in shaping the destiny of our nation as 1798. The patriots' names, the rebel songs and the places associated with 'The People's Rising' are an integral part of our culture. Our political family tree has its roots firmly planted in that period. All the parties who were involved in the historic Good Friday Peace Agreement, which paved the way for peace in Northern Ireland, have their origins back in that time. Co. Wexford was at the heart of the rebellion and consequently paid the highest price. From the Barony of Forth alone over three thousand were killed in the Battle of Ross. Estimates suggest that in just over a month at least twenty thousand Irish and ten thousand British lost their lives. Set in context this figure represents almost as many as were killed in the American War of Independence.

The Rebellion unfortunately became an opportunity to settle old scores and there was treachery, betrayal and profound bitterness. The amount paid in pensions to informers in today's terms amounted to nearly a €100 million, a figure which gives some indication of the extent of treachery involved. We can only wonder how many people from that time, and in the years following, may have gone to their deaths burdened with guilt, bearing deep resentments, and not at peace with themselves.

During the year of the bi-centenary celebrations 1998, I had the opportunity to celebrate Mass on or near many of the ancient battle sites. The requests to do so came from people living close-by who felt that the weight of the past still lay heavily on the present. At one such Eucharist two people remarked that a name they didn't recognize kept coming into their minds and with it a sense of someone needing forgiveness. For one it was the name Richards and with the other it was Lionel. The other participants could make no association with either name but one woman with a historical interest decided to do some research. Very quickly she discovered that the two names belonged to the one person. Lionel Richards was the name of the British commander who was responsible for some of the worst atrocities in that very area! Two hundred years later he had found an opportunity to ask for forgiveness.

Into the Light

Historical research can show that many areas that were associated with violence and bloodshed in the far distant past often became battle arenas at subsequent times throughout history. It would appear that history repeats itself in such places and in a very dramatic manner.

A couple moved into their new house in an area that was known to have strong connections with the Provisional I.R.A. Late at night strange noises and the sound of horses tramping outside would disturb them. They had searched for footprints but to no avail. The wife being of a more sensitive disposition than her husband, found that her energy drained while she was in the home and returned while she was elsewhere. Both of them sensed that something was seriously wrong, not so much with their new house, but with the area around which it was built.

They requested that a Mass be said in their home that would incorporate an attempt to figure out what might be the cause of such strange happenings. A local historian was invited who was able to fill in many of the missing details. The site was quite close to where a massacre had taken place during the Cromwellian period. It was also bordering one of the battle sites of 1798. Later, during the war of Independence in 1921, it witnessed a lot of violence with a number of particularly brutal murders having taken place nearby. It was obvious that psychic contamination of the area had been taking place over many centuries and this became the focus of prayer during the Eucharist.

During the celebration one participant was surprised to picture with her inner eye an individual dressed in uniform and carrying a Thompson sub-machine gun coming towards the altar. The historian present immediately identified the figure as that of Pax Sinnott who had been in charge of operations in that area during the period known as The Troubles.

This man's real name was Peadar but he had been nicknamed Paxo because later as a medical student he had made and tested a home made explosive for use by I.R.A. units while on active service. This unique mixture he called Paxo indicating that peace was the desired outcome. The Thompson sub-machine gun was known to be his favourite weapon and was like a personal signature leaving us in no doubt as to his identity. Around the county stories abound of men who incurred his wrath and found death without mercy from its bullets. Ironically Pax became a very successful doctor and practised in Wexford until his early death in 1957.

His entrance into the Eucharist came as a personal shock because it is to this same individual that I owe my very existence. After three days labour my mother was close to death and I was dangerously close to being brain damaged. Just when all hope seemed lost his intervention at the last moment in bringing about a safe delivery was always considered miraculous. It was a remarkable twist of providence to be welcoming the very person into the light of God who had first introduced me to the light of day.

Pax Sinnott
pictured on active service in 1921

A Road to Disaster

A stretch of road from Wexford to New Ross had become notorious for multiple and fatal accidents. Sometimes three, four or five people could lose their lives there in the space of a single month. It was a wide road and well maintained so there was no apparent reason why such accidents should be taking place. Approximately ten kilometers in length it stretched from an area known as Scullabogue to new Ross. The former was the scene of one of the most notorious and shameful atrocities during the 1798 Uprising where over a hundred people of Protestant stock were burned to death in a barn. This was an act of retaliation for the defeat by government forces at the infamous Battle of Ross. The area in between would have been part of the military activity of the time.

A resident of the area, who herself had narrowly escaped a potentially fatal crash, was discussing with her husband the alarming number of fatalities when he came up with an interesting insight. He observed that the most serious accidents tended to be head on collisions between British and Irish cars and often in the early mornings. Was it a case of history repeating itself with the present mirroring the past? The insight needed to be taken seriously and so a Eucharistic celebration was held in a house beside the road where the focused intention was to bring before the Lord for forgiveness and reconciliation all those who had been part of the ancient struggle and to pray a lessing on the area.

That happened in early 1998 when the bi-centenary celebrations of 1798 were just beginning. Would the accidents continue or would we witness a remarkable reduction? Looking back now after seven years there have been accidents but overall only two or three fatalities that stands in marked contrast to the same number and more that were losing their lives each month prior to the past being brought before the Lord.

A Troubling Episode

Thomas Cahill died under suspicious circumstances in 1923. He was interred in the old Cemetery at Cobh and his memory was suppressed because of suspected suicide or fratricide and also because he turned from the R.I.C. to the I.R.A. after 1916. He had been married to the local postmistress in a well to do suburb of the then Queenstown where many of the British military establishment resided. He was arrested in 1917 on suspicion of sheltering I.R.A. men and supplying arms. According to an obituary in the local paper he was one of the first R.I.C. men to turn after 1916. His wife at that stage was pregnant and had three small children. She was of British stock and being pregnant with three small children this would have come as a major experience of abandonment. In 1923 Thomas was released from prison but was now almost blind, allegedly as a result of being tortured. He received no welcome in his home and was last seen banging on the door in a drunken state. Shortly afterwards his body was found on the railway line under one of the near-by railway bridges. The next day his Brother in law left unexpectedly for the States never to return giving rise to the suspicion that Thomas may have been murdered.

Although these tragic events were never discussed, his Grandson accidentally discovered the details and found some amazing parallels with his own life which led him to the belief that there was 'unfinished business' in regard to his Grandfather. A Service was arranged near the spot of his death with family members present, together with a Sinn Fein representative. The group formed a circle of loving remembrance where the reality of this man's life was acknowledged after being denied for so many decades. His story was recounted in a compassionate understanding manner and this in turn gave way to the family offering forgiveness towards him and apologizing for the way he had been treated in the past. A sense of completion was experienced by all present, as if the final chapter of a book had been waiting for so many years to be written had now been done. For the family it was a connection with their past which had the power to reconnect them with each other in the present, a fact which became more and more evident in the months that followed.

Incarceration

By Donna Ansley

The story of Patrick Molloy is one of a man who was incarcerated in St. Ita's Mental Institution, Portrane, for over twenty years until his eventual death. It would appear that his wife and brother-in-law conspired to have him conveniently removed because a suspicion came to light that he had been previously married in Canada and also because Paddy had walked in on a 'scene' between his wife and that same man. The resulting rage was the evidence used to have him declared insane and locked away, leaving behind six young children.

It was over twenty years later that a telegram arrived to say that Patrick was on his deathbed. His wife Christina, now re-married, then relented and informed the family that all these years their father was not dead, as they had been told, but was in fact alive and living in Portrane. That evening all six grown up children and their mother stood around the bed of a man unable to acknowledge or recognize his own family in the last hours of his life.

There came a time in my life when I, Patrick's granddaughter, realized how strongly this man, who I had never even seen a picture of, was such a big part of my life. He represented all that was hidden and false, the hypocrisy, anger, shame and sense of injustice that have run through the generations and scarred my family. I began to seek ways to address these wounds and seek redemption for Patrick and his unacknowledged life. Also for his children and their children who were unknowingly carrying with them the scars of injustice and grief.

As part of this process an opportunity arose to tell the untold story and to bring Patrick into the light in the context of a Family Tree Eucharist that took place on May 4th 2006 in Kilmore Quay. It was the opening of a door to a soul that was finally coming home.

It was not uncommon from the 1850's to the mid 1940's for people deemed 'troublesome' to be incarcerated for life in mental homes for spurious reasons such as was the case with Patrick Molloy. These included domestic disputes, disagreements over land and being 'superfluous to requirements', as was often the case where a brother and sister lived on a farm and he decided to get married so his sister had to be 'conveniently removed'. Dispensary doctors signed the committal orders and while these were poorly paid they sometimes received handsome rewards for this particular service.

A Burning Issue

The Holocaust to Vengeance at the Wild Goose Lodge

By J.J. Tohill

Tuesday night Oct 30th, 1816 in the town land of Reaghstown in County Louth, a savage and murderous fire was raging. Patrick Devan, a local schoolmaster, and a man with an implacable thirst for revenge, had gathered a mob about him in his schoolhouse. Drugged with whiskey and threats he marched them under blazing turf sods to the lonely dwelling called 'The Wild Goose Lodge'. He had sworn to make a speedy end of the Lynches and Rooneys who lived there.

All around the house, Devan placed his men – there was to be no escape for the ill-fated victims. He gave the orders for bundles of straw to be thrown into the various rooms, and the blazing turf sods were to be flung in after them, resulting in one tremendous conflagration that seemed to redden the sky. The holocaust to vengeance had begun.

Vulgar and intoxicated jeering answered the hysterical shrieks for mercy from the doomed within the house. But nothing now could save them. Soon the fiercely burning roof timbers and thatch crashed down, and an ominous silence proclaimed that the night's dread work was over. When daylight came, between the blackened and gaping walls, eight charred skeletons were found; two of them were infants.

What prompted this terrible deed? The answer was simply revenge; it had its origin in a raid on the 'Wild Goose Lodge' a few months before. An unruly drunken mob were refused admittance by Lynch and Rooney, the mob had forced their way into the house, and in their search for arms accidentally overturned and broke some earthenware crocks that were used for storing milk for churning. The amount of the damage was minimal, about 80 cents On the following day a number of men, now sober, returned with a sum of money and apologized. It was indignantly refused. Little did they know that earlier that day Lynch and Rooney had gone to the local magistrate, lodged a complaint and given names of the mob?

Arrests followed quickly. Before night, three men, Tierney, Conlon and Shanley were taken prisoner. They were found guilty and duly hanged. It was a brutal punishment for the crime. Little damage had been done and at least one of the executed was known to be innocent. The effect on the people was profound. They spoke contemptuously of the law for in the hangings they saw nothing of justice. They branded Lynch and Rooney as traitors, and pointed to their dwelling with hatred.

There were those too who spoke of revenge and Patrick Devan spoke loudest of all. There were strange nightly meetings and speeches. Finally the blow fell. On that dreadful Tuesday night the countryside was lit up by that murderous fire and before daybreak hundreds had flocked to the scene. The soldiers in Dundalk barracks were all called out; every house within miles was searched. Specially trained policemen from Dublin were brought in and the manhunt of the century was on.

Yet it was not until four months later that Devan was arrested. His trial was speedy and the result was as expected. Two days later they sat him on a cart beside the hangman, and guarded by an escort of cavalry, took him to the ruins of the 'Wild Goose Lodge'. On arriving there he was promised his life if he would inform on his companions. He seemed not to hear. The sheriff asked his tragic mother to advise him, and she was lifted up onto the cart to his side. In a loud voice she cried out; 'Stag on no man to save yourself with the blood of any man.' She was rudely threatened and pulled down off the cart. Devan was then hoisted up and hanged between the remaining gables of the Lodge.

That same evening his body was cut down put in a gibbet and so placed that the setting sun would cast his dangling shadow on the door of his mother's cottage. For twelve months it remained there to haunt her days and nights. Other arrests now followed and a spirit of indiscriminate and irresponsible vengeance seemed to have taken hold of the authorities. They felt that somehow a salutary lesson must be taught to the country and if proper evidence could not be brought to light, men who made a trade in perjury could here and there be found. Ten men were arrested and indicted on such corrupt evidence and these were also hanged at the scene of the crime on March 9th. 1818. Their bodies were also left gibbeted all over the area for many months. By the summer of the following year, ten more swinging corpses added their ghostly creaking to the sigh of the wind, and the tragic tale of 'The wild Goose Lodge' had passed to the keeping of history. Or had it?

From the above account researched by J.J. Tohill it is very evident that such an event must have left an indelible imprint on the lives of that entire community. The legacy of bitterness and hurt would have been passed down from generation to generation. Sooner or later, given the right conditions, it was going to replicate itself and so it did.

On the 2nd of April 2002 the recently appointed parish priest of Louth was visiting an 87 year-old historian for the purpose of gaining information on the infamous burning of the Wild Goose Lodge. The old man was asking a question of the priest, 'Father do you believe in curses', when the telephone rang and his wife ran in to say that to say that Louth church was on fire. This had been one of the finest in the country and it was completely gutted. The walls were later tested and declared sound and so restoration began at a cost of 3.5 million Euro.

While attending a retreat in All Hallows College Dublin the Parish priest was drawn to an icon of Our Lady that was on display. It was just prior to the official opening of the renovated church and he enquired from the director as to the availability of the icon. His intention was to give it prominence in the new church. Not knowing where another might be available the Director presented the one he was using to the priest who proceeded to tell the story of the remarkable coincidence of the church catching fire from a blowtorch, which was being used on the gutters, just as he was being told about the torching of the Wild Goose Lodge.

Gradually the truth began to dawn. History had repeated itself in what had happened. The legacy of bitterness and resentment still needed to be healed. He had just been given the gift of a picture and now he could see that this was symbolic of his need to 'get the picture' of what was required. It was obvious that as soon as the church was opened, a service of healing and reconciliation was needed to put the past to rest and break the curse spoken of by the old man. Representatives from both sides of those involved would be invited, the story would again be told, apologies would be offered and forgiveness requested. The many who had lost their lives, and those who were responsible, would then be commended to the Lord. Thus would the dismembered be remembered and the age-old burning issue be finally extinguished.

The discovery of the story giving such a graphic account of the holocaust was itself providential. While the account was in still in its infancy and open on the computer I went to visit a friend at the opposite end of the country in Foxford, Co. Mayo. On several occasions while passing through an old hall- way my attention was drawn to a bundle of magazines lying to one-side. While saying farewell I spotted them again but this time picked out the one that was protruding the most. The first page that I opened was *The Holocaust to Vengeance at the Wild Goose Lodge*, written as if it were tailor made to complete the article waiting on the computer.

The Clare Island Story of Inclusion

During World War II the body of J.J. Tweed, a petty officer in the Royal Navy, was washed ashore on Clare Island in Co. Mayo, a place best known as the home of the warrior queen, Grace O'Malley or Grainne Mhaol. The body of the young man was found and brought ashore by local man Michael O'Grady to be buried. The priest on the island at the time refused to allow him to be buried in consecrated ground, no doubt presuming him to be of the Protestant faith, or no faith since he was from England! So, the man was buried outside the wall of the island cemetery much to the annoyance of Michael O'Grady.

The Good Friday Agreement of 1998 afforded the people of Clare Island the opportunity to demonstrate in some way their desire to redress the blatant sectarian stance taken by an earlier generation in their name. They knocked down part of the wall of the cemetery and rebuilt it, this time surrounding the grave of the young soldier. It was a deeply symbolic act of welcoming the stranger into their midst. The islanders were anxious to invite any of his living family members to the ceremony of inclusion of their long lost relative. The British Admiralty was contacted and it was found that J.J., known as 'Tweedie', was an orphan. Today he belongs to a big family who have taken him to their hearts in Clare Island.

J.J.Tweed's Grave
The inscription reads:
J.J. Tweed Petty Officer H.M.S. "MASHONA"
20th May 1944 Age 44

Our Faith Heritage

Cross of St. Mun

The above is a carved replica of the oldest Christian artifact in the Diocese of Ferns. The original was one of four which marked the boundary of an ancient monastery founded in the 6th Century by St Fintan who was also known as St. Mun. This was broken and desecrated by soldiers of the Cromwellian armies. An attempt was made to reposition the cross on its pedestal but it remains *The Broken Cross of St. Mun.* It is a potent symbol of the Christian faith and of its endurance through so many troubled centuries. It is situated near the entrance to the Church of Ireland in the village of Taghmon and its central feature is the symbol of the Diocese.

Spiritual Abuses

Bog Oak and Celtic Cross

The piece shown, made from bog oak, has been preserved in an Irish bog for at least four thousand years. As such it is a carrier of enormous history spanning the Christian era and also encompassing its Judaic origins. Nestling underneath is the Celtic Cross. Initially one's gaze tends to be drawn towards the larger bog oak sculpture but slowly the Cross begins to dominate the picture. The core of the Christian faith and its message has remained intact in spite of being overshadowed by enormous dark influences both historical and otherwise.

The Accretions of History

The Institutional Church is very much a product of its history and many practices and teachings in the past need to be acknowledged as abusive since they were so much at variance with the teachings of the Master. Even to this day many find the Catholic Inquisition incomprehensible and utterly scandalous. This was responsible for the publication of one of the most blood soaked books in human history called, *The Witches Hammer, which* indoctrinated the world 'to the dangers of free-thinking women' and instructed the clergy on how to locate, torture and destroy them. Those deemed as 'witches' by the Church included all female scholars, gypsies, mystics, nature-lovers herbalists and 'any who were suspiciously attuned to the natural world.' Even midwifes who used their medical knowledge to alleviate the pain of childbirth came under this broad umbrella and were hunted down and murdered. The suffering of childbirth was taught to be God's rightful punishment for Eve's disobedience in the Garden that gave rise to Original Sin. Witch-hunts extended over a period of three hundred years during which an estimated *five million* women were burned at the stake. This unsavory and violent piece of history effectively destroyed the contribution of female enlightenment and ushered in a period of imbalance characterised by male supremacy. The fallout from the Inquisition still exists in our churches today, especially in impoverished liturgies, where the role of the feminine is still unclear and greatly undervalued.

In the Irish context scandals might include:

Intolerance and prejudice towards other religious creeds. Catholics not being encouraged to associate with Protestants and not being allowed to enter a Protestant church or to attend protestant funerals. Often the impression was given that people of other religions were damned. It was not uncommon for the child of a mixed marriage to grow up tormented with the belief that one of his parents could never go to Heaven. Also, there was little or no openness to the truths contained in other faiths.

In the Gospel of John, Jesus describes himself as the Good Shepherd. A characteristic of the eastern shepherd is that he leads his sheep. Only when they are being brought to slaughter are they driven, not by the shepherd, but by the butcher! Preaching practice in the past emphasized the fear of God, and this fear of Hell, punishment, and eternal damnation was so often used to drive and control people without leading them into a genuine awareness of the love and mercy of God. An example of this was to be found in the catechism of fifty years ago where the question was asked 'Why do we attend Mass on Sunday? The answer children had to learn was, 'We go to Mass on Sunday because it is a mortal sin not to do so.' Many found that their experiences of religious leaders was akin to that of the Pharisees laying lots of burdens on people's shoulders in the form or rules and regulations but doing very to lift them. This resulted in so many being burdened by what has been classed as, 'Catholic Guilt'.

Our God Image

A family had invited some friends in for a meal. The conversation was continually interrupted by their four year who insisted on banging on the table with a spoon. Instead of taking the spoon away and scolding the child the father took the child on his lap and once secure in his father's love the child settled down and stopped his attention seeking behaviour. Such a view of God as Father stands in marked contrast to the image so often portrayed by the Institutional Church where God was presented as someone whose expectations of us were so high and whose opinions of us were so low that we always lived under his frown. The truth of God being pleased with us, his creation, of taking delight in us, of even smiling upon us was good news that was hardly ever heard. The legacy of this is that even today many have difficulty accepting themselves and few have come to experience the joy of being able to celebrate the wonder of who they really are.

The primary focus for Jesus was never on sin or morality. That was the preoccupation of the Pharisees. A genuine spirituality will of necessity express itself in good moral behaviour. Much old style religion was a question of do's and don'ts and mostly don'ts. The primary focus of catholic teaching was unfortunately much more on morality than on spirituality.

A story is told of two men who met in Hell. One asked the other why he was there and was told it was because he had committed murder. 'Well', he replied, 'You're lucky because I'm here for something that isn't even a sin anymore!' Particularly in the area of sexual sin, guilt was heaped on people who at the same time received no encouragement to appreciate the gift of their own sexuality. As a consequence of this, the only 'bad thoughts' someone could have were sexual. Having negative, bitter, resentful or vengeful thoughts were not afforded the same degree of seriousness.

The Book of Ecclesiasticus says, 'With humility have self esteem, and prize yourself as you deserve'. Jesus later taught 'Love your neighbour as yourself'. It would be true to say that the most overlooked word in the Bible may well be that little word 'as'. Instead of positive self-esteem being cultivated, people were almost encouraged to despise and see themselves as unworthy and even worthless. What a contrast to the teachings of St. Catherine of Sienna who could say, 'God gazed into the depths of himself. He so fell in love with what he saw that he had to create it. And so you came to be.'

Some practices amounted to blatant abuse. The humiliation suffered by poorer people in having money offerings read out from the altar. The practice of refusing Christian burial in consecrated ground to unbaptised infants and victims of suicide. The cultivation of the rich found shameful expression in the common saying relating to burial practices, 'High money high Mass, low money low Mass, and no money no Mass'

The practice of 'Churching' women after childbirth certainly did little to promote the sacredness of giving birth and fits into the general context of the victimization and demeaning of women which was rampant both in Church and society. Here echoes of the Inquisition still remained.

As in all cases where there is hurt, understanding paves the way for forgiveness and practices such as those mentioned above need to be viewed in their historical and societal context. At the same time such issues need to be named and the hurt must be acknowledged before a healing process can begin.

Tragic but True

The following tragic but true story is typical of so many more around Ireland where both Church and State were guilty of blatant, inhumane and inexcusable abuse against an individuals and families.

The year was 1948. Betty Quinn was seventeen when she became pregnant outside of wedlock. It was common practice at the time for such unfortunates to be sent to a Magdalene Home where her baby would be taken away, often to be reared as an orphan, and she would then spend the remainder of her days working in the laundry as a penance for her sins. Her parents, in spite of pressure from their local Parish Priest refused to allow this to happen and were happy to welcome the child and help bring it up as one of the family.

Going into labour in the middle of a cold November night she was brought by pony and trap to Tralee General Hospital. There she was refused admission because she was unmarried. She was then diverted to the poorhouse that was some distance away. On the way she had her child on the side of the road. Unfortunately there were complications, apart from the bitter cold, and both mother and child died on the spot.

Their funeral was brought to her local church where it was discovered that the local parish priest had put chains on the gates refusing her admission to the church or burial alongside her relatives in the graveyard. Officially it was because she was classed by the society of the time as a fallen woman against whom the gates of Heaven would be closed. The family had no option but to bury both mother and child outside the walls of the graveyard in unconsecrated ground.

Neither Church nor State had shown mercy either in life or in death.

Mixed Marriage

Captive Rings on Chalice

Peter came from a family where there was deep division going back to the marriage of his grand-mother, who was a Catholic, to a Protestant. It was a time when bigotry was rife and neither family approved of the wedding. Both sides refused to have anything to do with each other. The agreement was that the boys would be baptized and brought up as Protestants and the girls as Catholics. Considerable confusion was caused in the minds of her boys when it was revealed that their mother had secretly had them all baptized as Catholics just after birth. Peter therefore grew up, geographically quite close to, but at the same time not being allowed to associate with, one branch of his family tree.

Someone initiated a dialogue and it was arranged for a few interested members of both sides to come together and discuss how healing might take place. It was not enough for the present generation to agree to bury the hatchet, the roots also had to be dealt with. An important aspect of this, it was felt, should take place in the context of a liturgy with as many as possible of both sides being invited. It was quite obvious that the division was of an ancestral nature so one member of each family agreed to represent their side stretching through the generations, to acknowledge what had happened in the past, the hurt that was caused, and how contrary it was to the Gospel. An apology was then offered to the Lord and to the other side and forgiveness was requested. When the apology was received and the forgiveness granted both parties embraced and a gesture of peace and reconciliation was made between all the members. This represented both an end and a beginning, a closure of the past discord and an opening for the future to be lived in peace and harmony.

The simple formula outlined above has proven very effective in many situations where the roots of conflict go back several generations and it can easily be adopted and used in the context of a broader liturgy like, *The Family Gathering*, which is included in this book. Also a liturgy of this nature lends itself naturally to the use of symbols and with some creativity a very meaningful event can take place with far reaching consequences stretching back into the past and forward into the future.

PART 4
THE TIES
THAT BIND

Unresolved Grief of Parents for Lost Children

There are no Little Losses!

Celebrate Life – No Matter How Small

The pieces shown of a wine bottle and two goblets are made from antler. The Euro coin is included to give a sense of proportion as to their size.

What are the affects of unresolved grief in relation to miscarriages, abortions, stillbirths and child deaths and how can this grief be resolved? The loss of a child at any stage is a matter of deep hurt which until recent times went largely unrecognized and was rarely spoken about. Many adults are surprised to discover, often by accident, that they may have several more brothers and sisters lost through miscarriage or stillbirth that they never knew about simply because they were never mentioned. This is one area, which has opened up in the healing ministry in recent years with dramatic results. More and more people who all their lives struggled with a burden, which they could never fathom, are now finding freedom in the realization that their lives were unconsciously overlapped with a sibling who had died, but for whom the mourning process had never been completed.

How many are really in our Family?

The majority of people have lost a brother or sister. This is because of the frequency of miscarriage, abortions, stillbirths and twin loss. It is a medical estimate that as many as fifteen to twenty percent of pregnancies end in miscarriage, a figure much higher than was originally thought. Today as the abortion rate continues to soar, the number of stillbirths has diminished greatly. Up to forty years ago there were approximately two for every hundred live births; now the figure is down to approximately three per thousand. A far more amazing piece of research from the field of embryology indicates that one in eight of us were conceived with a twin. Many midwifery nurses have recently adopted the practice of examining the afterbirth for evidence of a twin from the early days of the pregnancy. In the majority of cases this search fails to reveal anything because modern photographic techniques can now reveal how in those early stages the tissue of the lost child can be absorbed by the one remaining. This means that only in the cellular memory of the remaining twin will any trace of the others existence be evident.

Miscarriages and Carriers

It seems to be a psychological fact that the unacknowledged and unexpressed emotions of a parent can be felt and carried by the child. Where a woman suffers a miscarriage she usually finds herself quite alone in her grief. In the eyes of society it is a small loss and even her partner, although he may be supportive, is unable to comprehend the extent of her loss. The result is that the natural flow of feelings, which would lead towards resolution, gets suppressed and while she manages to get on with her life those emotions don't go away. It may be the most vulnerable child or the one who is most dependent that now picks up on and becomes the carrier of the mother's feelings. Such a child begins to experience the world as a sad and lonely place and may even be programmed for a life of sadness. Having taken on the mother's sadness, he or she will most likely go through life taking on the burden of others' emotions wherever they go.

A Sad Beginning!

The next child to be conceived after the miscarriage or stillbirth may also be destined to marinate in the unresolved grief of its mother. Such a one may experience the womb as a morgue haunted with the feelings and vibrations of death. A child like this is very likely to be born with an innate predisposition towards sadness, pessimism and emotional fragility.

Poor Bonding

Another consequence of parents not having properly grieved a lost baby is that it will predispose them be emotionally unavailable to fully bond with subsequent children. Before a new child can be fully welcomed, the lost child must be grieved; otherwise the all-important sense of bonding with its parents will be greatly diminished. The feeling of 'not belonging' or an irrational conviction of 'having been adopted' seems quite common with such children. A comment from one woman in this regard was rather interesting: 'I am an only child and I arrived after three miscarriages and a stillbirth. You would imagine that I was greatly wanted and should have been greatly loved and cherished. Perhaps at some level this was true but it has not been my experience. I never felt close to either of my parents, particularly my mother. It was as if an invisible wall always kept us apart, to the extent that I often felt rejected by her. She's dead now, but I sometimes think that the grief which she never spoke about for her earlier children prevented her from being truly a mother to me, the one that survived.'

Imaginary Friends and Strange Attachments

It is not unusual for a child who has lost siblings to have imaginary friends, particularly if he or she is part of a small family, or where there is a significant age gap with other children. Very often such a child will tend to be a loner, shunning the company of other children in favour of these 'friends'. To the child these appear very real and often their names are known. Long animated conversations take place and coming to table, a place or places must be set for the 'friends'.

Usually after parents have handed over their children to the Lord, the imaginary friends disappear or are spoken of as 'having gone away' or 'gone into the light'.

It is not unusual also for a child to have a strange attachment to a doll or cuddly toy about which they feel anxious and responsible and having to account for at all times.

After a committal this attachment usually diminishes and other problems the child may have begin to show signs of improvement. From being a loner, relational skills develop, problems with hyperactivity lessen and where a child had learning difficulties, these begin to diminish and a new ability to concentrate ensues.

Light from the Dark Continent

In some African cultures there is a practice that stands in marked contrast to that of our Western society of not talking about and overlooking the significance of early losses. Where a mother loses a child through miscarriage or early death, the custom is to go to the local woodcarver who will carve a figure representing the lost child. This figure then is given a name and becomes part of the family. In this way the matter is always fully in the open and other children speak freely of their 'other' brother or sister. Only in very recent times have practices changed in maternity hospitals in relation to miscarriages and infant deaths. Up to this a mother was rarely allowed to see her dead infant before the body was buried in an anonymous grave in the hospital cemetery. It was common practice for the mother not to attend the burial. Today a more humane approach is taken which is much more conducive towards a proper grieving process. The mother is encouraged to hold her child, photographs and handprints are taken, a name is given, the death is registered and a proper committal service takes place with other family members present. All of this affirms the sacredness of life from the beginning and acknowledges that the pain of loss for the life that never will be need be, no less great than that felt for a life that was.

Limbo – A Marginal Issue

Something, which has caused unimaginable, suffering for countless parents down through the years, was the question of what became of children who died and who were not baptized? One belief was that they went straight to Heaven; but the much more commonly held one was that they went to Limbo. This was understood as a place where these innocent but unbaptized did not experience the pains of Hell but could not experience the fullness of God's love either. In other words Limbo was a state of natural happiness that excluded Heaven and the beatific vision.

The Roman Church has never condemned discussions on Limbo, but how did the concept arise in the first place? Saint Augustine, in reacting to one of the popular heresies of his day, backed himself into a theological corner where, in order to maintain his position he had to admit, albeit reluctantly, that unbaptized children, because they still carried the stain of Original Sin had to be condemned, but only to the mildest degree of punishment. Later Saint Thomas Aquinas argued against this position on the grounds that because a child was not personally guilty; it was therefore not deserving of any punishment. This gave rise to the suggestion that there might be another place for unbaptised babies, which was neither Heaven, Hell, or Purgatory. Some recent research of modern theologians such as Monica Hellwig seems to indicate that the whole idea of Limbo may have arisen out of a theological misunderstanding. This is what she has to say:

'The ordinary catechism and religious instruction have sometimes given a wrong impression as to what Limbo was all about. The word comes from the Latin 'Limbus' and means the margin or the periphery. As far as can be discovered the original discussions were about infants who died unbaptized before they had made any moral decisions. The original answer of theologians was in effect; 'We will have to place the question *in the margin because* we simply do not know'. Apparently by some confusion it came to be understood that it was the infants and not the question that was in the margin. Thus the 'margin' became a special place on the other side of death'.

Today there is a very welcome focus on the mercy of God and a strong emphasis on the role of the Christian community in bringing a child into the life of Christ. This approach acknowledges, at least implicitly, the importance of a proper grieving process in bringing a child into the fullness of life.

Where the Letting Go has Never Happened?

'Death breaks an earthly tie, but love survives when grief has passed, for love can never die'. The goal of the grieving process is the restoration of the love bond. Paradoxically this can only happen when all the other bonds of attachment have been severed. At this point only can there be a loving committal of the loved one to the Lord. A proper service may be an essential part of this process but it is unlikely that a final letting go can take place until much further down the line when the different stages of the grieving process have been negotiated. The fact that death may hide but doesn't necessarily divide then becomes a reality, and the doctrine of 'the Communion of Saints' takes on a whole new meaning.

Other Cultures and Customs – What can we Learn?

Rituals and beliefs throughout the world surrounding the death of children are rich and varied. Some in particular may have a lot to teach us. In the American Indian tradition it was believed that if a newborn child were named after a sibling that was lost, the spirit of the first would live on in the next. The practice of naming a child after another who died was widespread also in our own culture and may well have been responsible for imposing an intolerable burden on so many replacement children who could never be sure of their own identity since it was always overshadowed by someone else. Those unfortunate individuals who were often classed as 'being afraid of their shadow', may in such circumstances have had good reason!

Another interesting custom, which is often reported by missionaries working in parts of Nigeria where there is a strong belief in the Hindu custom of reincarnation, is that of breaking the finger of a dead child prior to burial. This is based on the belief that the spirit of this child is likely to reincarnate in the body of a subsequent child who will be recognized on arrival by having a bent or broken finger. Children are frequently born with such defects after the death of a sibling and are given recognition as their brother or sister having come back to earth.

Customs such as these and many others all indicate the possibility of a 'possession syndrome' where two identities can become so intertwined that the living one literally feels that he or she is possessed by another entity which is trying to live its own life in tandem through them. It is not uncommon for such victims to report schizoid tendencies, where they always find themselves trying to live two lives at once. It is understandable also why so many in this category find that they fight a losing battle in maintaining personal boundaries. At an unconscious level their boundaries are continually being infringed and this will inevitably find expression also in conscious life. This may well take the form of abuse, bullying, victimization and generally not being able to stand up for oneself and be assertive. The 'doormat syndrome' of continually being walked on is familiar territory for so many who suffer from this form of 'possession'.

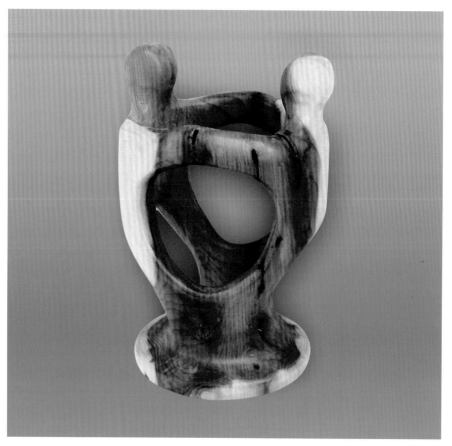

Ties that Bind

Sibling Bondage Scenarios

There are many possible scenarios that may give rise to sibling bondage. The harmful psychic link may be:

• To a twin, where the loss was at any age, from conception onwards.

• To a brother or sister who was miscarried either before or after them.

• To a child lost at any time becoming attached to most sensitive member.

• To a child lost through abortion that was never recognized.

- To a parent's brother or sister with whom they were identified.

- To a grandparent's child who was lost leaving an empty space to fill.

- To whoever they were unconsciously obliged to be a substitute for.

- To a child who died in the family that they were named after.

- To whoever they were considered to be the image of.

- To whoever others in family most closely associated him or her with.

Cutting the Ties

There are numerous visualizations that can be used for the purpose of cutting harmful psychic links. To use one or other in the presence of another person or persons seems to be very important. This gives the event an historical context and confers on it something of a legal status. It brings the decision away from the emotions to the level of the will with someone else present to bear witness to what has been done.

One technique, after having chosen a name for the child, is to visualize the person you feel attached to and yourself like two pieces of chewing gum. Both have been pushed together and then drawn apart leaving lots of stringy bits in between. Then visualize Jesus handing you a sword and with it begin to cut away all that is harmful between you leaving only a bond of pure love. You might gently reassure the other of your love but firmly state that the time has come for them to move on and for you to claim your freedom and be able to live your own life. You then visualize Christ walking towards both of you with arms outstretched and into his hands place the child you are holding. Next you ask the Lord to embrace this little one in his love and bring him or her into the fullness of life in his kingdom. There alone can they reach maturity and have all their dreams and hopes and expectations fulfilled.

Symptoms of Sibling Bondage

Continually feeling controlled – *Usually from both within and without.*

A victim of outside forces – *I easily fall into the victim mode.*

Poor sense of personal boundaries – *Personal space is not my own.*

High levels of stress and anxiety – *I am carrying a burden.*

Feeling over responsible – *I have been burdened with responsibility.*

Guilt/rejection/self-punishment – *I have only myself to blame.*

Anger at self and others – *I displace my anger at the wrong targets.*

Deep sadness – *Someone has never been acknowledged.*

Death wish – *Part of me at times wants to be with the other.*

Discontentment, nothing satisfies – *Something feels incomplete.*

Inability to cope with loss – *I am a bearer of unresolved loss.*

Sense of being two or more people – *Without being schitzoid.*

Feeling held back in life – *I need to deal with unfinished business.*

Difficulties with intimacy – *Transparency and sharing is difficult.*

Feeling unsupported in life – *I cannot even be there for myself.*

Not grounded in my own reality – *My reality is always shared.*

Imaginary playmate/s when young – *Especially where family is small.*

Codependent relationships – *Freedom is difficult because I am already tied.*

Psychic abilities – *I have a natural attunement to the unseen world.*

Eating disorders – *My lack of self-control in expressed through food.*

Restlessness – *There is something that doesn't allow me to find peace.*

Addictive tendencies – *There is an emptiness crying out to be filled.*

Isolation / Loneliness – *My inner self is divided.*

Fear of death or fascination with death – *I am linked with death.*

Overwhelming inner darkness – *This has a seductive quality.*

Difficulty with letting go – *There is something that has not let go of me.*

Sense of not belonging – *What I am linked to was never allowed to belong.*

Feeling different and apart – *Sense of being inwardly handicapped.*

Strong mother complex – *I am carrying some of her issues.*

Confused identity – *My identity is shared with another or others.*

Unstable self-esteem – *It always slips away from me.*

Sense of having a foot in both worlds – *I am linked to the other side.*

Confusion / Lack of clarity – *My life never seems to be my own*

Easily gives power away to others – *Psychically I am being drained.*

Carrier of other people's feelings – *Programmed from very early on.*

Poor concentration – *Scatterbrained or addicted to study as an escape.*

Often depressed before birthdays (Twin) – *Birth and death have overlapped.*

Deep psychic pain and inner struggle – *I know that something is not right.*

A mystery to myself – *There is a part of me I can never seem to reach.*

Feeling an outsider – *From the part of me that doesn't yet belong.*

Life energy being drained – *My life energy is being shared.*

Sibling Bondage – Quotes

'I felt as if I came into this world with someone else's soul to live out someone else's life.'

'I always thought that I should have been of the other gender, so I became a tomboy.' From a daughter born after the death of her infant brother.

'I seemed to be a disappointment to my mother.' From a 'replacement' child.

'I always seemed to be living between two worlds, the living and the dead.'

'It was as if my life wasn't my own and so I could never be myself.'

'I never could finish anything, yet I always wanted to.'

'I often feel as if I am not of this world.'

'I was strongly attracted to cross dressing.' From a man who had lost his sister very young.

'Whenever I tried to move forward something always seemed to hold me back.'

'As a thirty six year old I still have a teddy that I won't share with my nieces.'

'I felt that I was continually being haunted by spirits who were seeking attention'.

'I am a magnet for bad energies and dysfunctional people'.

'What others off-load I always end up carrying.'

'I seem to be living two lives and doing things by twos'.

'After puberty I became aware that I wasn't alone, that someone else was always with me.'

'I know that I was wanted at birth and yet I have always felt rejected.'

'Twenty years of having counselling and attending workshops have left me utterly frustrated; there's always a key piece missing.'

'Like the bit in the corner of the sardine tin, there's a bit of me I can never get at.'

'Whenever I leave home I feel as if I have left something important behind.'

'I am extra sensitive to vibes and subtle energies.'

'Loss and abandonment are key words in my life but for no apparent reason.'

'From the time I was a child I always wanted a baby sister. I didn't know that I had one.'

'I am vulnerable and have always played the victim role but can't seem to reverse it.'

'I am always searching for a missing part of me,'

'My brother and I were inseparable and often pretended that we were twins.'

'Dark clouds are never too far away on the horizon of my life.'

'I have always felt second best and could never find my place.'

'It's as if there's something that feels trapped inside me that wants to break free.'

'I don't know whether I belong to this world or the next.'

'I have lived my life always feeling that I've forgotten something.'

'Something is dragging the life out of me.'

'I feel as if I am being drawn towards death, yet I don't want to die.'

'For some unknown reason I have always been plagued with bad health.'

Post-Release Quotes

'After releasing my twin who died in utero I felt that I was on my own and able to be my own person for the first time in my life.'

'A weight that I had carried all my life was suddenly lifted.'

'My spirit felt light and free for the first time ever.'

'I experienced joy welling up inside and that was a whole new experience.'

'My facial and neck muscles have relaxed and I even look different.'

'I have always woken up with my fists clenched but now they're open.'

'My inner tension has dissolved and I feel a deep peace.'

'I was elated at first but then felt anger at my unjust imprisonment.'

'I feel as if *my* life is just beginning.'

'I feel grounded and with inner strength for the first time ever.'

'I am now able to be far more assertive and able to speak my voice.'

'My self-esteem always fluctuated but now it's much more stable.'

'I am now in charge of my life and am not playing the helpless victim.'

'Before part of me always felt rejected, but now I feel that I belong.'

'I always knew I was carrying somebody but couldn't put it into words.'

'My many years of inner work are now beginning to bear fruit.'

'At last I have some real understanding of myself.'

'At long last I'm free to be me.'

'My overwhelming cloud of sadness has evaporated.'

'The vital missing piece of the jigsaw has finally found its place.'

A Tale of Apples

Confirmations of Nature

Maria was twenty-nine years of age girl from Central Europe. She arrived in Ireland in response to an advertisement on the Internet offering work in this area. Like so many she discovered that the job was very different to what was advertised and that a large portion of her hard earned money was being demanded back by her employer as rent for sub-standard accommodation. One day while walking the road in floods of tears she asked the Angels to put her in touch with someone who could give her assistance. Passing by, I saw her distress, stopped the car and she got in and began to talk. It was obvious that the abuse she was being subjected to was affecting her health and this made it necessary to change her job from medical care to the only other work that was available in the area, which happened to be apple picking. Some time later, listening to the story of how her life had unfolded, it seemed obvious that she was once a twin. Some of the her tale indicators were as follows:

She was always searching for a part of her that felt lost.

Continually feeling used and abused.

Trying to move forward in life but always being held back.

Being plagued by bad luck and things not working out.

Having a bizarre pattern of near fatal accidents.

Holding an irrational negative reaction to her mother.

Having strong extra sensory perception.

Never wanting to celebrate her birthday.

Carrying an overwhelming sense of sadness.

Feeling haunted by lost souls.

Being very unsure of her identity.

Sensing that at times she was living two lives at different levels.

The strength of her reaction to the suggestion that she might have been a twin was itself indicative of that being the case. She admitted that her twin, a boy, had died at birth and she didn't even know if he had been given a name. The next morning with the twin very much on her mind she started her work in the apple farm. Reaching up to grasp for what she thought was one apple she was amazed to discover that it was a twin, as shown in photo. A week later, having contacted her mother to fill in the details and to decide on a name for the child, she cut the psychic links between them and handed him over to the Lord. There was an immediate sense of relief but it lasted only for days.

Next she began to wonder if the fact that her mother had a late miscarriage immediately after her might be another important key to unlocking her inner mystery. Perhaps the connection with her brother could have acted as a hook and facilitated a connection with this other sibling. Next morning she again reached up and picked an apple, this time to find that it had a smaller apple attached as shown. Once again she followed a similar procedure by naming and handed over this child to the Lord. This time she knew beyond a shadow of a doubt that something remarkable had happened. The heavy burden she had carried all her life was lifted, her spirit became light and she felt that she was able to inhabit her own space for the first time ever.

A week later she returned for a chat and produced the third apple shown in the picture. It seemed to hold significance but she wondered what? Perhaps it was that for a period she needed to exercise caution because the sibling severance may have left a wound that could leave her still vulnerable. This could result in looking to someone else to fill the void or picking up on negative energies from places or people. She needed to spend time on her own and be vigilant so as not to allow her new-found sense of identity to be taken away

The good news was that from there on her fortunes were reversed and her life took such a remarkable turn for the better that she could hardly believe it. The job of her dreams came her way; it paid well and within the year her goal of being able to return to Poland with enough money to build a home and get married was realized. In her own words she said, 'I came to Ireland with nothing and now I am going home with everything.'

Second Best

Looking back, my life has been like a jigsaw, with so many of the pieces just not making sense. Through many generations in my family, there has been a recurring pattern of illness and disagreements and in my own life there was a distinct sense of being 'haunted' in my home, and also of being a victim of outside forces that continually sabotaged my happiness and quality of life.

I was the middle child and the only girl in my family. Growing up I found myself longing and yearning for a sister I never had. Beneath my bubbly exterior, there was a deep sense of sadness and loneliness. It was as if I was always looking for a part of me that was lost. Hearing other girls complain about their sisters, upset me greatly as I considered what a great gift it would be to have a sister. Only as an adult I found out that I did actually have a sister who died shortly after birth, and also two other siblings who were miscarried. How these losses were still impinging on my life has taken me most of my life to discover.

I grew up in a home which was no stranger to hardship and grief. My father died at forty-four and my mother at fifty-four. Both had suffered very bad health for years. From the age of 18 my life became plagued with medical ailments. Something was weighing me down and interfering with my life, even to the point where I wondered if I might be possessed? On so many occasions, I remember praying, and asking God to remove this person or 'thing', which was so difficult to live with. At some stage also I realized that so many of my sicknesses were mimicking my mother's complaints and this was a good indication that I was still carrying unresolved issues around her death. In adult life I faced this issue of unresolved grief, but in spite of my best efforts there remained something unresolved, a big part of the jigsaw was still not in place.

All my life, for some reason I felt 'second best'. Once my husband gave me a lovely necklace for my birthday. Instead of being pleased my reaction was one of hurt and rejection simply because it was only rolled gold and not the real thing. Another part of me felt guilty because not only had it cost a lot of money, but he had also taken great care in choosing it. While attending an inner journey workshop in we were challenged to take note of our reactions and then look for connections between what we were experiencing then, and what had been our experience in the past. Later that night I lay awake and began to reflect on my life. The necklace issue in particular came to mind; why had it caused me to go over the top? Connections began to come to mind; rolled gold was not real gold so it was second best. That feeling was very deep inside me and so it felt as if my husband was treating me as second best. I was second in the family, and being born prematurely only eleven months after my brother again left me with similar feelings. While musing on this, a face began to float around in my mind; it was that of a little girl I had never seen before. She bore a striking semblance to a photo of me taken when I was about seven. Suddenly I realized that I had known this girl all my life. She was the person whose presence I had felt all these years. In fact I knew her nearly as well as I knew myself. It seemed plausible that through my mother's grief, our lives had become overlapped with her's, overshadowing mine. No wonder my feelings of being second best had been so intense and also why I still felt so unfree of my mother. Clearly there was a harmful connection between myself and my sister that had to be broken. I spoke to her, and told her that it was wrong for her to try and live her life through me, and that it was time for her to move on. I sensed something coming loose between us, followed by her moving into the light. Having handed her over to the Lord in this way, I felt both relieved and elated. A sense of peace came over me, and during the next few weeks the atmosphere in my home that had so often felt strange, became more peaceful and calmer than I had ever known it before. Even my children, who knew nothing of what I had done, remarked on this, and how pleasant the home now felt. A most important piece of the jigsaw has finally found its place, and now with a sense of my own identity, a body that seems to be getting healthier by the day, for the first time, I am enjoying living 'my' life.

Sibling Dream

Rena was having great difficulty coming to terms with the death of her grandchild. He was born prematurely and lived just a few days. The intensity of her grief, even months after, made her feel that it carried a deeper dimension. She had a recurring dream where she found two letters from her mother in the postbox of the front door of the house where she grew up. They seemed to have been there for a considerable time. One was addressed to her and the other to her daughter who had lost the child. Exploring the symbolism of the dream it was obvious that three generations were involved and a message was being passed down from the older to the younger. The postbox could easily be associated with the womb and the letterbox as the entrance. The fact that it was the front door seemed to point towards the future. Drawing all the strands together it appeared that something of importance from the past needed to be known in the present and dealt with in a manner that would clear the way for future generations. The grandmother had lost four children before birth and was known never to have come to terms with those losses. Then it was her only daughter who was born next that also lost a child before full term. Now it was the granddaughter who was suffering. It appeared that the unresolved grief of one generation was passing as a harmful and destructive legacy down through the generations and this was the message that needed to be received, acknowledged and healed.

In this case the mother needed to acknowledge the grief she had carried all her life from her mother and then cut the harmful psychic associations with death between them. This in turn should open the 'door' for fruitful pregnancies in the next generation.

The Light that Conquers Darkness

A 'Nutty' Candle

The following story may seem to belong to the, *Ripley's Believe it or Not,* category. However, it was witnessed by the two people involved and is told exactly as it happened.

Nicola was born eighteen months after her mother had given birth to twin boys, one of whom had died. As a child she was bright, intelligent and exceptionally gifted in poetry, drama and music. Even then she sensed that there was something wrong. From as far back as she could remember she had always wanted a baby of her own. Then one Christmas she asked for a black doll which she named Rachel. This became her constant companion and accompanied her even into later life.

As a teenager she became troubled and disruptive both at home and at school. She developed a morbid fascination with death and the occult. Her strongest reactions were to women in their thirties, especially when she was under their control. They in turn found her most difficult. As a young teenager she dabbled in drugs, got involved in strange relationships and made several suicide attempts.

At seventeen she sought help. The issue of attachment to her brother was identified and dealt with. This made sense of why she had always wanted a baby. In effect she was always attached to one. Cutting the ties with her brother brought a measure of freedom but the work needed to go deeper. She then remembered that all her life complete strangers would call her by the name of her doll, Rachel. Gradually she sensed the presence of a woman in her thirties, a quite troubled soul, who was trying to live her life through her. While her brother-attachment was in place she had never detected this presence whose name she believed to be Rachel, even though the earlier one was probably acting as a hook for the second.

A candle was lit to symbolically welcome Rachel into the light. The moment Nicola said, 'I see her but she is in great darkness,' the candle immediately went from full flame to zero. There was no smoke, which later made me wonder if some minute spark had remained in the wick. Fifteen minutes or so later as the ties being cut were nearing completion Nicola sensed Rachel asking forgiveness for trespassing so much on her space and preventing her from living her own life. Just as forgiveness was being offered a tiny flame appeared on the candle as if out of nowhere. A few minutes later Nicola said that she was seeing two angels conducting Rachel into the light. Just then the candle burst into a flame almost double its normal height. However one might interpret such a strange phenomenon it reflected very accurately and confirmed the deeper reality of what was taking place.

The girl in the above story wrote the following poem. It is an attempt to express her inner reality before and during the process of recovery.

Yours Truly

Trying so hard to reclaim what is yours,

A feeling of loss and so insecure,

Knowing that you were never in charge,

Something mysterious always at large.

Wondering where the next the feeling would lead,

Hours of emptiness sorrow and need,

So many roads yet all incomplete,

Not knowing why you would always retreat.

Something not fitting, and yet seeking place,

Losing each thing you held in heart space,

A hopeless feeling of spanning a divide,

Desperately wanting to turn back the tide.

A heavy burden weighing you down,

Feeling so close you could almost drown,

Sensing that so much was always at stake,

Not knowing if your body would break.

Patiently waiting, feeling the pain,

A slow opening up and attempt to explain,

Hoping I wasn't just going insane.

Clarity dawning, each day a new gain.

Take all the insights, hold onto them tight,

Rebalance your life with all that is right,

Open your heart, take the journey to whole,

With courage and hope let your true self unfold.

Just take back now what is rightfully yours,

No longer are you to feel broken and used,

Complete your own task and state your own views,

Control your own life and remember you choose.

Telling Stories

A Brother Substitute

Leonie was eight when her mother expressed concern that there seemed to be something troubling her daughter. She was always very insecure and clung to her mother to an inordinate degree always fearing that she might be left on her own. As she got older there were no signs of her growing out of this dependency. At times she acted like she was depressed and would often say to her mother that she felt as if she were lost and was very sad, but didn't know why? Two years before Leonie's birth her little brother had died just a few weeks after he was born. The mother admitted never having grieved properly for that child and was advised to have another child to help come to terms with her loss. Throughout Leonie's pregnancy she naturally thought continuously of the child she had lost, but kept working intensely to avoid the overwhelming feelings of sorrow. The next child absorbed the mother's unexpressed grief. At a deep level she was a substitute for her brother and had the bond not been broken would have grown up with a major crisis of identity plus a host of other symptoms associated with sibling bondage.

Here it was the mother's perception that the unresolved loss of one child was impacting on the other. In fact she had been advised to substitute one in place of the other.

Loss and Intimidation

John was having problems with being bullied in work by his supervisor. Other members of his team could stand up to this man but for some reason, not John. The death of his father ten years earlier seemed to be a big unresolved issue in his life. He admitted to never having let go of his father but sensed that there was a deeper reason as to why he was unable to do this. His elder brother had died a year before he was born and it made sense that as a child in the womb he would have been subjected to his mother's feelings of grief and anxiety. This early association with loss would have made it difficult for him to deal with losses in later life. Similarly the emotional onslaught he experienced in the womb would have left him vulnerable and with a tendency to avoid emotional issues in later life.

In this case the death of a sibling left someone vulnerable, prone to anxiety and fear and finding it difficult to integrate loss as a part of life.

Male Overshadowing

Moya's birth was overshadowed by her brother's death. He had died shortly after birth and her mother had been advised to have another child to 'get over' her grief. At eight she was sexually abused and at twelve she was raped. This happened on five other occasions until she was twenty, when she got married. She had two children and for the next seven years lived in terror and was often brutalized by her husband. She left and went to live in another part of the country but was only there a short time when a man broke in to her house and raped her. Not long after she fell deeply in love with a man who seemed to be the answer to all her dreams but within a few months he died in her arms of a heart attack. A few years later she took up with another man who asked her to collect some parcels from a railway station. En route she was arrested for carrying a large quantity of drugs and spent several months in prison with her children being taken into care. Returning home she found that her house had been taken over by squatters and left in a terrible state. There followed years in prostitution but eventually she broke free and met a very kind and considerate man. Her current problem was that her past was still haunting her and she was driving her new partner away from her by allowing so much hurt and anger from an earlier time to spill over into this relationship.

In effect most of Moya's troubled life could be traced back to her brother's death. Always overshadowed by the male she had been a victim of the male all of her life. Only by cutting this harmful psychic link could a process of recovery begin.

A Forgotten Sister

Penny was an attractive, very intelligent, nineteen year old university student who had been suffering from severe bouts of depression. The death of a school pal seemed to have been the trigger but was not the underlying cause. She described her depression in terms of feeling that she didn't belong, that no one cared, that she felt lost and utterly alone. An intolerable sense of sadness, where she could cry inconsolably for days, was also part of her experience. She had repeatedly fantasized about her own funeral but nobody ever turned up and no one even noticed that she had died. Her mother who was present was asked if she had had another child before Penny? There was an earlier girl who had died at birth. This had happened during a time of stress and upheaval and she was forced to return immediately to work. No attention had been given to the grieving process and the child had never been given a name. Her husband had never mentioned the matter and although the lost child sometimes came to mind she rarely spoke about her. Occasionally she admitted wondering if the unresolved grief in regard to that child could have any bearing on Penny's behaviour? The description Penny had given of her symptoms and fantasy seemed to indicate that there was a significant psychic overlap between herself and her unmourned, unnamed sister and that this, most likely, was the main cause of her depression. The manner in which her life unfolded after the ties had been cut seemed to indicate that this was in fact the truth.

Quoting from a letter received from the mother some months later: *'A wonderful healing has result-ed not only for Penny but also for myself. It is such a gift to see her laughing, happy and at peace with her-self. She is now beginning to make plans for her future and what she wants to do when she finishes college'.*

It would appear that the reality of the lost child, whose death had never been acknowledged, was being expressed through Penny in her darker moments.

Distance Healing

Sandra came for counselling with certain physical and emotional problems that were causing her concern. Among other things her blood pressure was dangerously high and she was putting on weight for no apparent reason. In discussing her past history she said that her mother had had four miscarriages and one of them had occurred when as a baby she was being bathed by her mother. We discussed the necessity of naming those children and giving them recognition. The following week we arranged to have a Mass said for those miscarriages.

Almost immediately after the Mass Sandra's health returned to normal and she experienced a renewed sense of well-being. An even more remarkable effect was the complete healing of her mother who had been seriously depressed for over twenty years. This woman lived several thou-sand miles away and had no knowledge that a Mass was being celebrated for her four children. Her recovery happened quite suddenly much to the amazement of her doctor. She felt so well that she was taken off all medication and her recovery was lasting and permanent.

Such a knock on effect for other family members who are totally unaware of what is taking place is a common feature of this kind of ministry. Such happenings underpin the reality of how the fami-ly system is so interconnected.

A Witch's Story

Olive was in her mid thirties and deeply involved in witchcraft. All her life she had been depressed had made several suicide attempts and had been on medication since the age of eleven. Her moth-er exercised an inordinate level of control in her life and Olive felt that she never had any sense of her own identity. Feeling so controlled and not having any religious background she turned to witchcraft in an attempt to find answers and reclaim some power. Her mother had had an identi-cal twin who had died at eleven. Olive was named after this twin whose loss her mother had never come to terms with. The recognition of what had been happening, even before any ties were bro-ken, brought Olive into a level of peace that up to this she had only dreamed of.

An Unresolved Murder

Leanne was a middle-aged woman who had searched deeply for answers and spent long periods in counselling. Her first marriage was very abusive and she only managed to break free after the violence became life threatening. When her three sons grew up she remarried and moved to another country. This was deeply resented by her adult sons who became verbally abusive and sustained their barrage over many years. Her new husband also became more and more abusive and difficult to live with, leaving her very isolated.

Some months before she was born, Leanne's aunt had been murdered by her husband. This had deeply traumatized Leanne's parents who over the years tried to shut out the memory of such an awful event. The second name they gave to Leanne was that of her aunt. At a deep level, from the time she was a child in the womb, Leanne had carried the unresolved trauma of that event and the pattern of her life seemed to be a replication of what had befallen her aunt. In the process of cutting the ties she remarked that the one person she had always wanted to meet was her aunt, while at another level she had always known her.

Abortion

Amanda was a five year old who from the time she could talk seemed to be in communication with an invisible entity or friend she called 'Polly'. This was a name that had never been used in the house. Her mother, Teresa, was unmarried and became pregnant as a result of being taken advantage of by someone at a time when she was very vulnerable. Her initial reaction was to have the child aborted and had made arrangements to do so until a friend asked the question, 'Is this really you?' Something about this question that could be taken at many levels caused her to change her mind and continue with the pregnancy. Two years after the birth an aunt who the mother was named after, died This woman Teresa kept repeating the words, 'Pray against abortion' as she was dying. This was in spite of not knowing anything of her niece's story. Investigation revealed that there was another Teresa in the previous generation. This woman had died at thirty-six and her death cert revealed that the cause of her death was, 'Septicemia resulting from an abortion'. From piecing together the scant details of her life it would appear that although married she was not sexually involved with her husband and had an affair with another man. When the pregnancy resulted she was then forced into having an abortion using a very primitive and unsafe method. An even more amazing part of the story was that this woman was known always not by Teresa but by her nickname, which was Polly!

It would appear that Polly had a special interest in the child who, unlike her own, had escaped abortion. As soon as she was prayed for, the child stopped calling the name Polly.

PART 5
PRAYERS &
RITUALS

Teach us to Pray

In response to their request to teach them to pray Jesus taught his disciples the *Our Father.* The following is a prayer that has arisen out of a similar request; 'Lord teach me to pray'. It has become central to my prayer life over a number of years and expresses the disposition of surrender, openness and listening to Spirit that is necessary in order to become truly instrumental in Family Tree Healing. It is not offered as a formula of words to be recited but rather a way of life to be embraced.

Prayer of Surrender

Lord, I place my life in your hands,
I entrust myself to your care,
I acknowledge you as my Lord and Saviour,
Master and Redeemer.

I choose to live out of your abundant riches,
And to draw from the storehouse of your infinite wisdom.

Help me to hear what you want me to hear,
To say what you want me to say,
To know what you want me to know,
To be where you want me to be,
To do what you want me to do.

I commit myself joyfully to your work,
Knowing that your power working in me,
Can do infinitely more,
Than I could ever ask, dream or imagine.

Don't let me get in your way,
And don't let me die until my work is done!

To you O Lord be the glory,
The honour and the praise,
Through all generations,
Amen.

The Eucharistic Celebration

Cutting the Ties

'Do This as a memorial of Me'

Intergenerational Healing needs to be understood as a process which demands, and should be given, considerable time. Truth often comes to meet us half way when we are willing to meet it, but it often leaves us waiting! The Celebration of the Eucharist while it is quite central comes never at the beginning, but at the end of the process when issues, which need prayer and attention, have been clearly identified. Only when the jigsaw is as complete as possible, particularly with the missing pieces in their rightful place, should it be placed on the altar. The Eucharist then, while it is a remembering of the 'faithful departed', can also incorporate an apology for the 'unfaithfulness' of departed ones as well. Those who have never had a proper Christian committal can then be commended to the Lord. Where an injustice was a major part of a family history and people died with bitterness and resentment the surviving members can now stand 'proxy' for them and offer forgiveness on their behalf. In the words of Scripture 'It is a holy and wholesome thought to pray for the dead that they might be freed from their sins' (2 Macc.12:45) It is not unusual that over a period of time, and often with remarkable suddenness, someone in the present and even an entire family may find a new level of freedom as well.

The following is a Eucharistic Ritual that may be shortened and adapted by the celebrant for particular situations. It contains the format and prayers that have evolved over many years of ministry.

Intergenerational Healing – The Eucharistic Celebration.

Greeting and Introduction.

May the Lord be with you and all those who have gone before us, especially those of past generations that we remember in prayer.

We gather in the presence of the Lord, the one who is the same yesterday today and forever, the sovereign Lord of history. We submit ourselves and all those that we pray for under his Lordship, asking that he might be their King and Lord, Master and Redeemer. We claim the protection of precious blood for all both here and beyond the veil who will be touched by this liturgy and we ask that our thoughts prayers and actions will be guided by the inspiration of the Holy Spirit.

In celebrating the Eucharist we are proclaiming the Lord's death. In other words we are making present his death both to the seen and unseen world. This is the celebration where time, as we know it, ceases to exist and we are one with him as his life is given on the cross for the salvation of the whole human race. In that spirit we ask the Lord to send his holy angels to the four winds to bring to this place, which is also the foot of Calvary, all those souls who, for whatever reason, have not been free to go the journey and find their rightful place in God's Kingdom.

Christ promised that the Spirit would lead us into all Truth. This is not just the truth about himself and the Father but it can also be the truth about ourselves and of our ancestry. We pray for openness to that truth which enables us to understand what is the root cause of some of the struggles in our lives; what is it that prevents us from being fully who we are and prevents us from enjoying the liberty of the Sons and Daughters of God?

Sin opens a door to darkness, which only Repentance can close. A central part of a Family Tree Liturgy is to offer an apology to God on behalf of those who have gone before us.

Penitential:

Father, in the name of your Son Jesus, we apologize and ask forgiveness for our own sins and the sins of all of our ancestors living and dead, in the family trees of our fathers and mothers and in the generations of the Church. I invite you to bring to mind the surnames of your father's and mother's families.

Father we apologize for any occult involvement or practices that may have been carried on by any of our ancestors. Any door that may have been opened to Satan in this way, we ask that it might be closed and in the name of Jesus we bind up any evil influence which may hold people in bondage and may still be passing down our bloodline.

Many people feel that their families were the victims of a curse or curses. We now apologize for and cancel by the blood of Jesus all curses, from any source, which were directed against our fore-bearers and on their behalf we forgive those who were responsible.

We apologize for the unbelievers in our family trees and for all sins committed through ignorance, deception, arrogance, pride, rebellion, lawlessness, rudeness and stubbornness.

We apologize for those who were drug addicts, gamblers and alcoholics and for the suffering they inflicted on others.

We apologize for all the unforgiveness bitterness and resentment, hatred and revenge, all dissention and division between members of our family trees and between the different Churches.

We apologize for all the fighting over land or money or material possessions or power. For all greed, envy, jealousy, corruption, for all the evictions of people from their land and houses.

We apologize for all our ancestors who were involved in war crimes, oppression and violence and who may have used their positions of authority through the power of the gun. Also for any torture or unjust suffering that has been inflicted on others, any brutality, cruelty or terror mental, physical, spiritual or social.

We apologize for all those who were involved in lies, stealing, bribery, perjury, dishonesty, insincerity, compromise, cheating, and oppression of the less fortunate.

We apologize for all those who have been involved in promiscuity and sexual perversions, those who have sexually abused others, those who have been involved with pornography and prostitution, those who have allowed sex to be the governing force in their lives.

We apologize and ask forgiveness for all the children who were aborted and denied the opportunity of life. For all who assisted in performing abortions and for all suicides and self-destruction.

For all parents who never did, or never could, take responsibility for their offspring, for the hidden pregnancies and the countless individuals who, in never knowing or being recognized their parents, were deprived of so much of their own identity.

For the black sheep and all who were disowned by their families because of shame, many of whom were locked away in mental institutions.

For all in our families who were least loved in life and least mourned in death, those not spoken about and the ones who died unreconciled with their families.

For all who suffered sudden death, who may not have had time to make their peace with God, others, or themselves. For these and all who died with unfinished business.

For all who died in exile, were drowned at sea or killed in war; for all who did not receive a Christian burial.

On behalf of those who have gone before us who died with bitterness and resentment, we now choose to forgive those who were responsible for those hurts and injustices inflicted against them.

Opening Prayer:

God our Father it is your will that none of your children should be lost but that all would be saved and come to the knowledge of the truth. May the eternal truth of your infinite love and mercy reach down through the generations, redeeming the past, releasing the present, giving hope for the future and bringing all those that we pray for into the fullness of your eternal life and love.

Offertory Prayer:

In a spirit of faith and love we bring our family trees to your altar Lord. With this bread and wine may they be transformed. May all souls be washed clean in your blood and come into their right place of communion in your Kingdom.

Sign of Peace:

Jesus calmed the storm on the Sea of Galilee saying 'Peace; be still'.

In our own lives, in the history of our family, in our Church and in our nation we have experienced many kinds of storms. At this time in our Eucharist we proclaim the peace of Christ into all of these.

So, in the name of God our Father we say 'peace; be still' to all experiences of trauma, panic, fear, turmoil, terror and violence, in our own lives, in the life of our family, of our Church and of our nation. In that same spirit we now share the peace of Christ with each other.

*Closing prayer:

Merciful God, it is not for us to judge anyone who has died. Rather we come to you with the assurance of your great compassion. We unite with our wounded brothers and sisters and believe that you draw them to your forgiving heart. May the love we bear be encouragement for all souls winging their way home to you. Thank you for your unconditional love for all you have created.

Shorter Penitential Form:

We unite with all souls who have died and who may not yet be at peace. (Certain individuals may be named prayerfully).

.... those who have taken their own lives or caused their own deaths.

.... those who died due to violence or brutal aggression.

.... those blinded by ambition and who were greedy and dishonest

.... those who failed to reconcile their anger and remained alienated.

.... those who have been executed for the crimes they committed.

.... those who fought death and refused to be comforted.

.... those who lived in loveless marriages where resentment smoldered.

.... those who used and abused others for their selfish pleasure.

.... those whose cruel actions brought suffering and death to others.

.... those killed in car accidents and as a result of recklessness.

.... those who died from alcohol and substance abuse.

.... those who raged against others and died with hate in their hearts.

.... and any other souls who died in distress for whom we wish to pray.

Eucharistic Prayer – Love

Blessed are you God of tenderness and compassion, revealing your great love in the warmth and affection of human life, and in the gentleness and sensitivity of nature.

Blessed are you God of love and unity, forever inviting people towards peace and reconciliation, towards friendship, closeness and intimacy.

Blessed are you God of loving surprises, sending us Jesus to bind up the wounds of human loneliness, drawing us closer to one another in a love that lasts forever.

With all who share in the call to love, people on earth and all the celestial beings in the heavens, we sing forever our song of praise.

Holy, Holy, Holy…

God of love and tender compassion, you seek to draw together all that is scattered amid the sadness and fragmentation of human failure, and the pain and destruction of human greed.

You seek to restore creation to its original wholeness so that all creatures, great and small, unite in the loving and creative harmony of life.

Your Spirit never ceases to reconcile all that fragments, and to unite all that divides. That same spirit awakens our hearts and quickens our imagination, as you invite us to grow into the fullness of life and love.

We now ask you to pour out your Spirit on these gifts of bread and wine, so that they may become food for our pilgrim journey, to nourish and nurture us on our way.

On the night before he died, Jesus, having loved us unreservedly, and with a total generosity of heart, gave us his own life through these humble gifts of bread and wine.

Taking to himself the bread, he held it lovingly, and offered it to his friends with these words: 'Take this all of you and eat it; this is my body which will be given up for you. Do this in memory of me.'

He then took the cup of wine poured out to be shared among friends. Gratefully and lovingly he offered it with these words. 'Take this, all of you and drink from it; this is the cup of my blood, the cup of the new and everlasting covenant. It will be shed for you and for all, so that sins may be forgiven. Do this in memory of me.'

Let us proclaim the Mystery of Faith.

As we celebrate this sacred meal, we call to mind all you have shared with us through the gifts of creation, and especially in the gift of Jesus our incarnate Lord, who loved us so much that he gave all he had, even the gift of life, that we may be free to grow deeper into loving fellowship.

As we recall this love from ages past, we look forward as the Kingdom unfolds and the reign of Jesus – in justice, love and peace – becomes established on the earth.

May the Spirit who transforms all life, renew us afresh as we share this sacred food, so that we become agents for growth and change in a world yearning for the love and peace of the kingdom.

We pray for those here present and all whose lives bring hope to our world. Lord of the living and the dead, awaken to the undying light of pardon and peace all those who have fallen asleep in faith, especially those who have died alone, unloved and unmourned.

We celebrate this Eucharist, united in heart with all who seek God, in the various creeds and cultures of our world. We rejoice with all who share the fellowship of faith – living and dead – and we open our hearts to all who seek the truth.

One day may we be united with the family of humankind, set free from bondage and sin, so together we can praise and glorify the God of all peoples, who forever gathers the scattered flock into the unity and love of the Kingdom.

Through Him, with Him, in Him…

Prayer for Liberation from an Inherited Burden

Father of mercy ………….. is your son/daughter from even before his/her conception. You know what his/her needs are and everything that weighs heavily upon him/her. Therefore I ask you to undo every negative burden in the life of ………………

Lord Jesus you came to save us. Your blood was shed for our salvation. May that blood fall mightily upon the mind of …………… cutting all the links with evil that are hidden there and allowing him/her to put on the mind of Christ. Undo every negative hereditary burden that weighs upon ………… particularly any form of curse, addiction or occult influence. May your brother/sister be freed by the power of your Redeeming Blood.

Holy Spirit, your light can penetrate the most profound depths of our being, healing us from all evil. I ask you to powerfully shine your light upon …………. freeing him/her from bondage to anyone living or dead and from every snare, stumbling block and trap of Satan.

May God be praised and adored in the life of ………… May he/she be free to walk in your ways, live the life that you have marked out and give you glory.

Amen.

Prayer for Liberation From a Curse

Lord Jesus Christ

I believe that you are the Son of God who died on the Cross for my sins and for me you were resurrected from the dead.

With faith in your Cross, and in the finished work of Calvary as my foundation, I believe that all the powers of Satan arranged against me have been broken.

Therefore I entrust myself to you as my Lord and Saviour and claim the protection of your Precious Blood. In the authority of your name I oppose any force of darkness and particularly any curse that has come into my life – either by my own acts, from my family or ancestors or any other way that I am not aware of. Wherever there are any dark shadows in my own life or affecting that of my family I now renounce them and forgive anyone who has wished evil upon me, my family, or upon those who went before me.

I refuse to believe any longer in the power of any curse that has been influencing my life or that of my family. In the mighty name of Jesus I sit in judgment over all the forces of evil that have tormented us. I detach myself and my loved ones from all that is negative, oppressive or destructive and I claim absolute freedom from their power.

I call on the Holy Spirit to take me over completely and fill my heart with divine love. May all my thoughts be positive and pleasing to him and may that same Spirit keep me free from all evil as only the Spirit of God can do.

Amen.

Family Gathering – Prayer Service

*Gathering Prayer

Gatherer of all good memories,
the spirits of many ancestors join us in this sacred place.
We have come here to celebrate a family history,
to gather the memories, good and bad, of many generations.

You have been a companion for each one,
every grandfather and grandmother,
every father and mother, brother and sister, son and daughter.

You have been the breath of life for everyone who has
birthed a child, wedded a lover, or buried a dear one.

You have sown the seeds of deep faith in the waters of countless baptisms,
and that faith has been kept alive in this family for hundreds of years.

Today we take hope and find courage in what we celebrate,
the strong faith of our ancestors that sustained them through the difficult times
of evictions and hardships, troubles and woes.

We give thanks for the support of neighbours and friends,
the leadership of priests, the goodness of each one willing
to reach out and be there in time of need.

May we be filled with hope, through this celebration, knowing
that this family believed in your constant presence,
accepted your grace, shared your love
and celebrated your life with one another.

*Remembrance Prayers

Response: 'Be with them O Lord'

We remember those who lived fully and loved deeply.
Those who found the source of their inner strength in you O Lord.

We remember the light-filled ones who kindled our spirits with the spark of their beliefs,
their teachings and wisdom.

We remember the brave ones who walked through their struggles with hope
and taught us to have confidence in times of sorrow and difficulty.

We remember the vulnerable ones who allowed us to care for them
and to be with them in their time of need.

We remember the risk takers who faced their fears and took action
even though they had to pay a heavy price.

We remember the faith filled ones who brought us, through words and example,
to a deeper relationship with you Lord.

We remember the nurturers who birthed us physically or spiritually
and gave us sustenance by their caring presence.

We remember the great lovers of life whose humour and enthusiasm lifted our spirits
and brought us joy.

O God, giver and sustainer of life, we thank you for all those that we have known
and loved and those we have never known but whose lives have touched ours and
in a mysterious way have helped make us who we are. May our lives model their virtues
and may our hearts resonate with their goodness.

Concluding Prayer:

Father we pray, that the love we celebrate today in this Eucharist may always hold us together
as one in your family.

That our bonds of affection may extend beyond time and space, embracing those
who have gone before us and those who will come after us.

That nothing negative may have power over us.

That our mornings may be filled with strength and that the evening of our lives will find us gracious and fulfilled.

That we may have the courage to live our lives to the full.

We ask this through Christ our Lord.

Final Blessing:

May the nourishment of the earth may be yours. – Amen

May the clarity of light be yours. – Amen

May the fluency of the ocean may be yours. – Amen

May the protection of the ancestors be yours. – Amen

May Almighty God bless us all. In the name of the Father, Son and Holy Spirit.

AMEN.

Prayers in this chapter marked with an asterisk are taken from *Out Of the Ordinary* by Joyce Rupp. Used by permission of Ave Maria press. All Rights reserved.

Ancora hupero – I'm still being

Bibliography
and Recommended Reading

Healing the Family Tree	Dr Ken McAll	Sheldon Press, 1982
Healing the Haunted	Dr. Ken McAll	Darley Anderson, 1989
A Guide to Healing the Family Tree	Dr Ken McAll	Handsel press, 1994
Healing Your Family Patterns	David Furlong	Piatcus, 1997
Genograms in Family Assessment	M. Goldrick & R. Gerson	Norton & Co, 1985
The Presence of the Past	Rupert Sheldrake	Fontana, 1989
Quantum Healing	Deepak Chopra	Bantam, 1989
Twins	Peter Watson	Sphere, 1984
Cutting the Ties that Bind	Phyllis Krystal	Weiser, 1993
Healing Your Family Tree	John Hampsch C.M.F.	Sunday Visitor, 1986
Intergenerational Healing	Robert DeGrandis S.J.	De Grandis, 1989
Until Today	Iyanla Vanzant	Pocket Books, 2001
Bless Me Father	Eamon Kelly	Mercier, 1977
Restless Spirit	Margaret Hawkins	Mercier, 2006
Understanding Trauma	Janet Thornton	Thornton, 2003
Remembering	F.C Bartlett	Cambridge, 1992
Out of the Ordinary	Joyce Rupp	AMP, 2000
Invisible Loyalties	B oszormenyi Nagy	New York, 1984
The Ancestor Syndrome	Ann Schutzenberger	Routledge, 1998
Ghosts & Earthbound Spirits	Linda Williamson	Piatkus, 2006
The Lost Secret Of Death	Peter Novak	Hampton Roads, 2003